Bicycling Michigan's Northland in 2013

Bill Bacheler & John Correll

Fulfillment Press
Canton, Michigan

Bicycling Michigan's Northland in 2013: A Pictorial Story of Two Senior Guys Who Bike-toured Michigan's Picturesque Eastern Upper Peninsula for a Week in 2013

Fulfillment Press
Canton, Michigan

Copyright © 2013 by John Correll and Bill Bacheler

All rights reserved. No part of this book may be reproduced or transmitted in any form or by any means, electronic or mechanical, including photocopying, recording, or by any information storage and retrieval system, without written permission from the author John Correll, except for the inclusion of brief quotations for review. Any clipart used in this book is copyright material of Microsoft Corporation.

Printed in the United States of America.
ISBN: 978-1-938001-15-4 - paperback | 978-1-938001-87-1 - hardcover
Version: TXT – 2013-10-20(6)   COV – 2013-10-20(4)

Bill's Dedication: To my wife Pam, who cheerfully put up with the time I spent training for this bike tour (instead of doing my household chores). And, thanks to Dave of Soo Pro Sports, who kept my old Ross 10-speed in excellent operating condition.

John's Dedication: To my wife and life partner Janet, who challenged me to take my first bicycle tour, which I did in 2009.

Purchasing Info
To buy a copy of this book, please visit either Amazon.com or a retail outlet that sells books on bicycle touring or Michigan travel.

Publicity Info
For an article or interview for your magazine, Internet blog, or radio or television program, contact: publicity@correllconcepts.com

Other Books
For info on other books and publications by John Correll, visit: www.correllconcepts.com

Contents

Introduction 4

About the Writer and Photographer 5

How the Tour Came About 7

~ Day 1 ~ Sault Sainte Marie to DeTour Village 9

~ Day 2 ~ DeTour Village to Trout Lake 24

~ Day 3 ~ Trout Lake to Blaney Park 42

~ Day 4 ~ Blaney Park to Munising 56

~ Day 5 ~ Munising to Grand Marais 69

~ Day 6 ~ Grand Marais to Newberry 101

~ Day 7 ~ Newberry to Sault Sainte Marie 115

~ Afterward ~ 138

If You Seek a Pleasant Peninsula, Look about You. — **Michigan's State Motto**

Introduction

***It is by** riding a bicycle that you learn the contours of a country best, since you have to sweat up the hills and coast down them. Thus you remember them as they actually are, while in a motor car only a high hill impresses you, and you have no such accurate remembrance of country you have driven through as you gain by riding a bicycle.*

*— **Ernest Hemingway***

In this passage Hemingway describes a special aspect of bicycling: the experiencing and remembrance of the landscape over which one travels. But, there's even more to it than that. When you travel by bicycle, *and* you do it with a certain curious mind, embracing spirit, and an eye and ear open to the world, your experiences and remembrances of the *entire journey* are different from what results when traveling by car. These experiences and remembrances can derive from everything you encounter. They can come not only from the terrain but also from the temperature of the air, the direction and speed of the wind, the sun and the rain and the sky, the surface of the road, the plants and animals and businesses and abodes that line the road, the sights and sounds of nature and of people working, playing, and traveling, and, finally, they can come from other beings who intersect your life in that time.

When you bike in this way you're not just performing a recreational activity or merely going from here to there, you're experiencing the world in a different way, in a way that's outside what one experiences when traveling enclosed in a self-propelled capsule. It's a way that enables you to stop and examine something more closely, to take it in a little longer or experience it a little more thoroughly, and, of course, to forever capture the memory of it in a photograph.

This book aims to portray that type of biking experience, as it transpired for two senior men who bike-toured a portion of Michigan's Upper Peninsula for seven days in August 2013.

Cycle tracks will abound in Utopia. — ***H. G. Wells***

About the Writer and Photographer

John and Bill (left and right) in front of their motel room in Newberry before "hitting the road" on the last leg of their weeklong bike tour of Michigan's beautiful Eastern Upper Peninsula (August 2–8, 2013)

JOHN CORRELL performed the writing, formatting, and publishing functions for this book. So we've dubbed him "the writer." A senior of 69 years (in 2013), John resides in Canton, Michigan with his wife Janet. He's a self-employed writer, publisher, inventor, and business consultant. His main business entity is Correll Consulting, LLC. In addition to biking, some of his other pursuits include walking, fishing, and Michigan/U.S. travel and sight-seeing.

BILL BACHELER created most of the photos in this book. So we've dubbed him "the photographer." A senior of 68 years (in 2013), Bill resides in Sault Sainte Marie, Michigan (a.k.a. the Soo) with his wife Pam. He's a practicing dentist and is a partner in Sault Dental Associates. In addition to biking, some of his other pursuits include wood boat-building, camping, and cross-country skiing.

Note: The word "sault" is a Canadian French word for rapids or waterfall. It's pronounced "sue." As a side note, Sault Sainte Marie — also spelled Sault Ste Marie — is one of the oldest continuously inhabited communities in the U.S. It holds a number of noteworthy attractions, including the Soo Locks. For more info, visit www.saultstemarie.com. Also, just for your information, there's a Sault Ste Marie in Ontario, Canada. It's right across the river from the U.S. Soo.

The Two Peninsulas of the Great State of Michigan

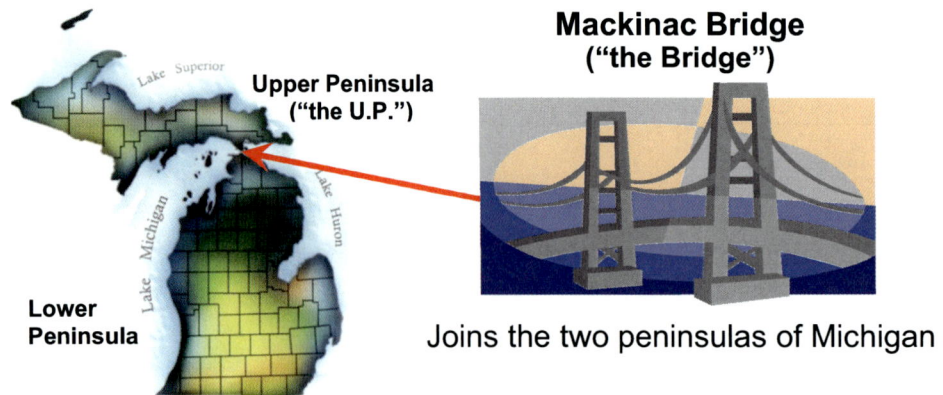

Joins the two peninsulas of Michigan

Eastern Half of Michigan's Upper Peninsula

The 2013 Bike Tour Itinerary
August 2–8, 2013

DAY 1 = The Soo to DeTour Village (**1**) – 70 miles

DAY 2 = DeTour Village to Trout Lake (**2**) – 74 miles

DAY 3 = Trout Lake to Blaney Park (**3**) – 52 miles

DAY 4 = Blaney Park to Munising (**4**) – 66 miles

DAY 5 = Munising to Grand Marais (**5**) – 51 miles

DAY 6 = Grand Marais to Newberry (**6**) – 53 miles

DAY 7 = Newberry to The Soo – 67 miles

How the Tour Came About
August 2–8, 2013 ~ 7 days, 433 total miles

It was August 2008. Janet and I had been married 41 years, and I was now 64 years old. We had just finished visiting Tahquamenon Falls in Michigan's Upper Peninsula, commonly called "U.P." And, were now heading south on Highway 123, on our way home.

We first visited the Falls in August 1967 on our honeymoon. We'd been back three times since (yes, it's that good). A few miles south of the Falls on Highway 123 we passed a couple cross-country bicyclists. As we did I wistfully murmured, "Years ago I used to dream about doing that."

There were a few seconds of silence. Then Janet uttered a statement that caught me fully off guard and, in a way, changed my life. She looked at me and said, "So, what's stopping you?"

I had no answer. In 1979, at age 35, I started bicycling. I've done it every summer since. In the first 15 years or so I thought it would be cool to do some multi-day cross-country touring. But as the years passed and my body slowly aged I forgot about it — took it off my bucket list. So, after searching my head for an answer to Janet's vexing question, the only response I could muster was a feeble "I don't know."

But the question kept rattling around in my brain for the next two weeks. Finally I couldn't take it any longer. One day after returning from a bike ride I announced that I had decided to do a one-week bike tour.

The first words out of Janet's mouth were "Who are you going to do it with?"

I replied, "No one. I'm doing it by myself. I don't know anyone else who bikes."

"Well, okay," she said, "but I wish someone else was going with you."

About a week passed. Then one day while on a walk I realized that I did know someone who bikes. It was Bill Bacheler — a friend from boyhood and long-time resident and prominent dentist of Sault Sainte Marie, Michigan (he's a partner in Sault Dental Associates). So I sent Bill an email asking him if he'd like to do a weeklong bike tour in summer 2009. I told him I figured we'd be doing 60 to 70 miles per day. His response came back the next day. "This sounds interesting. But I'm not certain I'm able to get myself in shape for it ... but I'm willing to try."

I told him those were my sentiments, too. At the time Bill and I were doing bike rides in the 20 to 25 mile range. So we both had a ways to go to reach 60 to 70 miles per day. We decided that if each of us could build up to at least a 40-mile ride by the time the colder weather came (around October), it would be possible for us to get in good enough shape to complete a 7-day, 400-plus mile tour at the end of next summer.

The next summer we each worked diligently from April through July at getting into shape for our planned excursion. And then, August 8–14, 2009, we did a 7-day, 434-mile bicycle tour of Michigan's Eastern Upper Peninsula. The departure and destination point was Bill's home in Sault Ste Marie (the Soo). Our route comprised the following: Day 1 — The Soo to DeTour Village; Day 2 — DeTour to Trout Lake; Day 3 — Trout Lake to Blaney Park; Day 4 — Blaney Park to Munising; Day 5 — Munising to Newberry; Day 6 — Newberry to Paradise (10 miles south of Whitefish Point); Day 7 — Paradise to the Soo. We slept in motels, as opposed to campgrounds, because we figured it would make a more enjoyable experience.

When we departed on August 8 neither of us was certain we'd be able to pull off this "crazy venture." But on August 14 at tour's end, when we finally pulled into Bill's driveway, it was with no small measure of joy and satisfaction that we had, indeed, done it. During that time Bill had taken many photos and we had amassed a cache of unforgettable memories. That evening the inevitable questions arose: "Should we do this again next year? Should we do it again *ever?*" We both had tired legs. And, Bill had sore wrists and neck and I had a sore butt. Plus, the conditioning for and actual doing of this tour had required hundreds of hours of riding time by each of us. Basically, this undertaking had involved each of us scheduling nearly our entire summer around it. So, as regards the question "Should we do it again?", we made no decision on it. Subsequently I wrote an account of the trip and published it with Bill's photos on my website. I also published a private paperback book of the experience, which we gave to family and friends and which Bill even included as reading material in the waiting room of his dental office (which he has reported is the favorite read of many of his patients). But beyond that we never made the book available for public sale or viewing.

Three and a half years passed. Then one cold snowy evening in January 2013 the memory of the trip popped into my head. I pulled the book from the bookshelf and began leafing through it. Then a strange thing happened: I got an urge to *do it again!* The next day I sent an email to Bill, which in essence said: "Hey, how'd you like to do another one-week U.P. bike tour this summer? You can take all the photos you want and I'll put them into a book, like I did in 2009, except this time we'll make it available for *public viewing.* I'll submit it to Amazon, and perhaps even to bookstores, for the world to read." The next day Bill's reply came back: "Yes, I think I'd like to do it again. And I especially like the idea of this time creating a book the entire world can see." So, to follow through on my promise to Bill, *this is the book*.

Two Notes

1 – Itinerary. Our day-by-day tour itinerary is shown on page **6.** As it turned out, the first four days traced the same route we took in our 2009 trip. The last three days took us to "new ground."

2 – Photos. Most of the photos, and virtually all the best ones, are Bill's handiwork. For the fun of it I also took a few. Photos from Bill's camera are indicated by a **"B"** in the photo number (the number at the top of each photo). Photos from my camera are indicated by a **"C"** in the number. Also, just for the heck of it I've included a few of the best 2009 photos (most of which were taken or set up by Bill). These photos are indicated by a "P" and a "2009" in the photo number.

~ Day 1 ~
Sault Sainte Marie to DeTour Village

DATE: Friday, August 2, 2013

LUNCH STOP: Main Street Café (in Pickford)

ROUTE: Bill's place to Riverside Dr (in the Soo) — Riverside Dr south to 22 Mile Rd — 22 Mile Rd east to Pennington Rd — Pennington Rd south to Gogomain Rd — Gogomain Rd west to the town of Pickford (lunch) — Gogomain Rd east to Raber Rd — Raber Rd south to North Caribou Dr — N. Caribou Dr east to DeTour Village

LODGING: Huron Street Inn (in DeTour Village)

TOTAL MILES: 70

I had taken the 6-hour ride from Detroit to Sault Sainte Marie on Thursday, August 1. Bill and his wife Pam provided me with a comfy bedroom so we could start early Friday morning. I made the trip in my Ford Focus. So I had to slightly disassemble my bike to fit it into the vehicle. In carrying my bike this way I inadvertently disarranged my front brake. So Bill and I spent time after dinner that evening adjusting the brake back to proper operation. We set our departure time for the next day to be 10:00 a.m.

We arose the next morning at 7:30. Bill prepared us a hearty breakfast of oatmeal and juice.

At 9:30 Jeff Lozen arrived. Jeff is an optometrist who resides in the Soo (and is a partner in Sault Vision Clinic). Bill had extended him an invitation to do the tour with us. Jeff couldn't take off the entire week, but opted to ride along with us on the first two days: Friday and Saturday.

At 9:45 — 15 minutes before scheduled departure — rain began and thunderstorms rolled in. If it were only precipitation we would have left at the scheduled time. But we had lightning, quite another matter. After about 20 minutes the lightning passed, but the rain continued. We spent the next half hour analyzing the Internet weather map trying to figure out if we might be able to dodge the rain by waiting a little longer. We finally concluded that getting wet that day was part of our biking destiny. So we set out on the first day of our weeklong U.P. bike tour at 11:00 a.m., with rain spanking us in the face.

A journey is a person itself; no two are alike. And all plans, safeguards, policing, and coercion are fruitless. We find after years of struggle that we do not take a trip; a trip takes us. — **John Steinbeck, Travels with Charley**

Left to right — Bill, Jeff, John in Bill's garage (the birthplace of Bill's beautiful handmade wooden watercrafts, including row boat, kayaks, and canoes).
We had given up waiting for the rain to end and, so, we departed in the wet stuff about three minutes after this photo was taken by Bill's wife Pam.

Like three wild-wheeling teenage boys we weaved and dodged our way via side streets, sidewalks, and parking lots for five miles through the city of Sault Ste Marie, until we reached Riverside Drive, and there turned southward. Gradually diminishing sounds of far-off thunder rumbled in the distance. The rain welcomed us to the great U.P. outdoors as we pressed onward. And it would continue to do so for the next two and a half hours.

Virtually every biker considers rain to be a downside. But the weather this day did carry an upside: a moderate backwind for virtually the entire way.

At about the one-hour mark we made our first and only "mis-turn" of the trip. One of us misread the directions, interpreting "22 Mile Road" to be "12 Mile Road." And so we wrongly turned down 12 Mile Road. After about a mile we realized our mistake and backtracked. It only added an extra two miles to the day's travel, no big problem.

About 30 minutes before reaching Pickford, our lunch stop, a teensy patch of blue sky appeared on the southwest horizon. It's funny how such an insignificant sight can produce so much euphoria. Anxiously we watched this blue patch as it grew. Soon, azure sky, white clouds, and sun were everywhere — and the rain nowhere! So Bill took the opportunity to capture a couple photos, the first of over 300 that he would take in the next seven days.

B269

**Jeff and John (l-and-r) pressing southward after two and a half hours of rain.
But good news is on the horizon — blue sky and white clouds are emerging.**
(Note the hay rolls — a.k.a. hay barrels — they're all over this area of the Upper Peninsula this time of year.)

B272

We encountered a goat family in a pasture.
This little fella found Bill and his camera fascinating. (Maybe he thought Bill had some billy-goat treats for him, or maybe he just likes having his picture taken for a book. Too bad he'll never have opportunity to read it.)

Eventually we reached the small town of Pickford and our lunch stop: the Main Street Café. Before having lunch we took the opportunity to shed some water and "dry out a little." (Jeff left, John right) John wringing out his socks.

We discovered that our delightful waitress Linda happened to be a semi-pro fishing angler. This triggered much conversation.

Day 1 | Sault Sainte Marie to DeTour Village

Linda explained that she and her dad enter major fishing tournaments as a team. Just a month prior they had come in *fourth* in the Cabelas St. Mary's River walleye tournament. Considering the number of fishermen in such tournaments, fourth place impressed us. A week after the end of our bike tour Bill and Jeff went to a weigh-in of another Cabelas tournament at the Soo. To their surprise they encountered Linda and her dad, who were there for the tournament.

(L-to-r) Bill, Linda, Linda's not so happy son, dad Paul, and Jeff in the parking lot at a Cabelas fishing tournament at the Soo. (Note the graphics on the truck.)

Two handsome diners enjoying nourishment provided by the Main Street Café in Pickford.

Day 1 | Sault Sainte Marie to DeTour Village

One of the things we planned to do that evening was attend a production of the play *Oklahoma!* by the DeTour Village Players. This poster in the Main Street Café lobby reminded us of our exciting upcoming evening agenda.

Soon we got back on our bikes. Following are some photos taken on Gogomain Road as we traveled eastward on our way to DeTour Village.

John riding with a chintzy plastic pancho he purchased in a general store in Pickford for $1.50. He bought it as preparation for possible rain which appeared to be coming from the west. The pancho didn't work; it tore apart in the wind. But for a few minutes it provided a humorous "Superman cape," which gave us more than $1.50 of laughs.

Day 1 | Sault Sainte Marie to DeTour Village

B284

Ominous rain clouds begin to appear once again. For over an hour we traveled along the edge of a rain front. Eventually we encountered the wet stuff, but not as heavy as before lunch.
Note the hay rolls in this photo and also other photos, such as B269. It's an important crop in this area.
Each summer Pickford holds a special Pickford Hay Days festival around the end of July.

B289

John getting out the rain cover for his carrying bag.
(That's another goat herd in the background. But they apparently didn't give a darn about Bill and his camera.)

On our 2009 tour we passed this humorous spot by the side of Gogomain Road. We decided we just had to have a photo. So we set up this one with Bill in it. We dubbed it "Yooper Rest Stop."

Here's how it appeared almost exactly four years later, on August 2, 2013 (with Bill in it again, of course).

Terminology Note for Non-Michiganders: The State of Michigan comprises two peninsulas, called Upper Peninsula and Lower Peninsula. Michiganders typically refer to the Upper Peninsula as *the U.P.* and refer to the fortunate folks who live in the U.P. as *Yoopers*.

Eventually we came to Raber Road, which took us southward, and then to N. Caribou Dr, which took us eastward to DeTour Village. Following are photos of a few interesting sights on the way.

"Antler House" — no mistaking its purpose.

Creative art using an old tree. We'll dub it "Yooper sculpture."

Hey, still enough room for at least one more Rocky Point resident.

A couple sandhill cranes looking for dinner in a hayfield (presumably easier to do than looking for a needle in a hay *stack*). This majestic bird populates Michigan's Upper Peninsula during summer, and migrates south for winter.

Along the way we encountered sporadic sprinkles of rain. By 6:00 p.m. we finally arrived at our destination, the Huron Street Inn, located in the small waterfront community of DeTour Village. The Inn is a charming B&B owned and operated by local residents Dave and Susie Rhinard. We stayed there on our 2009 tour and had a good experience, so opted to do it again.

B22(2009)

A welcomed sight, indeed, after six hours in the saddle, with about half of it in the rain.

B23(2009)

Our room — the "Carriage House" — was second floor of the white garage. Although it might look small in this photo, it's actually a spacious rustic facility that was perfect for the three of us.

After we arrived at DeTour we spotted this rainbow. We took it to be a sign of good luck.
This waterway is known as DeTour Passage. It's the south end of the St. Mary's River, where the river empties into Lake Huron. The far shore is Drummond Island. Coincidentally, we saw this sailing vessel about 10:00 a.m. that morning as it was entering the north end of the St. Mary's River at the Soo (in front of Bill's home, which is on the River).

Jeff (left) taking a photo of the rainbow, with Bill watching (or perhaps supervising, photographically speaking).

Day 1 | Sault Sainte Marie to DeTour Village

Soon after we arrived at the Huron Street Inn we discovered that the musical play *Oklahoma!* — which we wanted to attend — started at 7:30. Fortunately it was just a couple blocks away, in the gymnasium, or "performance center," of the local high school. We hustled to get ready and then walked down the street to the DeTour Village Inn, a popular local eatery. We didn't have time for dinner so we quaffed a beer and did the short two-block walk to the high school.

DeTour Village Inn — one of several good places for a bite and a beer in DeTour. (Photograph taken next morning)

Stage bows after the *Oklahoma!* grand finale. (Note the 4-person "orchestra pit" in front of the stage.)
As it turned out, this production of *Oklahoma!* was one of the most enjoyable, memorable plays I've ever experienced. All three of us found it to be a perfect end to our first biking day. The tall fellow in the middle with the cowboy hat was main character Curly, played by Marshall Werner who's a chemistry professor at nearby Lake Superior State University. He's about 6'10" tall. The tall woman (in his left hand) is one of his daughters, a high school student. He's also a fishing buddy of Jeff's.

Day 1 | Sault Sainte Marie to DeTour Village

Even though the main street of DeTour Village is just three blocks long and even though you may have never heard of DeTour Village Players and even though the entire orchestra comprised just four instruments (piano, piccolo, clarinet, and percussion), the set, acting, singing, and instrumental music of this production was *first rate* — totally professional, thoroughly enjoyable. Interestingly, the stage director was Dave Rhinard and the stage manager was Susie Rhinard, owners of the Huron Street Inn (where we stayed). Dave also performed in the play as traveling salesman Ali Hakim. Yoopers are versatile folk, indeed.

After the play we went back to the Detour Village Inn (photo B326, prior page) for dinner. It was now 10:30. Even though we ate cookies during intermission at the play, we still were famished. The Inn was packed with others from the play. But we managed to find a table in a corner at the far back of the room. Finally the bartender/waitress came over (the place was very busy and she was running around hectically). To our disappointment, she informed us that the kitchen had closed at 10:00, but we could get a bag of chips. So we ordered a couple

Day 1 | Sault Sainte Marie to DeTour Village

bags of chips and a round of beers. We gobbled down the chips and quaffed the beers and then left, hoping to find some place that sold food. But, being a very small town, the only place that was open that had food to eat was the corner gas station/convenience store, the DeTour Express Market.

Fortunately the Express Market was stocked with a wide selection of grab-and-go foods, and had a microwave to heat it in. We picked out what we wanted, heated it up, and ate it standing in the store. The store cashier — the sole employee there — graciously assisted us in proper use of the microwave and made sure we had all the condiments and eating accoutrements we needed. We got back to the Carriage House (which was the "attic" to the garage, and just down the street from the Market) by 11:30, quickly went to bed, and slept soundly all night, until 7:30 wake-up time the next morning.

Inside the Carriage House (John left, Bill right)
We hung up our wet clothes to dry out, using about anything we could find for a hanging device, including the ceiling fans.

~ Day 2 ~
DeTour Village to Trout Lake

DATE: Saturday, August 3, 2013

LUNCH STOP: Hessel Grocery Market (in Hessel)

ROUTE: Hwy 134 west to H63 (also called Mackinac Trail) — H63 south to Hwy 123 — Hwy 123 northwest to Trout Lake

LODGING: McGowan's Motel (in Trout Lake)

TOTAL MILES: 74

The day opened with beautiful sunny skies — no more rain. But it would turn out to be the toughest day of the trip, not because of the 74-mile ride but because we rode against a vigorous headwind for all but eight miles of it. Breakfast this morning was scheduled to start at 8:30 a.m. So at precisely 8:30, Bill, Jeff, and I made the 30-foot walk from the carriage house to the back door of the main house, through the kitchen where Dave Rhinard was cooking, and into the dining room. The table, splendidly set, awaited our arrival.

The breakfast plate, featuring "chef" Dave Rhinard's mouthwatering pizza frittata, was graciously served by hostess Susie. (The ingredients for the vegetable garnish, if I recollect correctly, came from their garden.)

The menu included the delicious, eye-opening pizza frittata (Dave Rhinard's creation and name), fresh fruit platter, orange juice and pineapple juice, sourdough bread toast, raspberry jam, and salsa. The salsa, jam, and sourdough bread were *homemade* by the Rhinards, with some of the salsa ingredients being from their home garden. And all of it was beautifully presented and tasted great. The three of us "chowed down" and relished every moment of it.

The best part of the breakfast was that we got to chat with hosts Dave and Susie about their B&B and the prior evening's fabulous production of *Oklahoma!* As previously mentioned, Dave was the stage director of the play and also one of the main characters and Susie was the stage manager (definitely no shortage of energy, versatility, and creativity with these two).
L-to-r: Jeff, Dave Rhinard, Susie Rhinard, Bill, John — in the dining room of the Huron Street Inn B&B.
For more info on this delightful B&B, visit www.thehuronstreetinn.com.
For info on DeTour Village, visit www.detourvillage.com and/or www.detourvillage.org.

Getting ready for travel this morning took a little longer than usual. First, we oiled our bike chains (which were beginning to "stiffen" from the prior day's rain). Second, packing — at least for me — required a little extra time due to the partially wet clothes from the prior day. And, lastly, we couldn't resist visiting a couple local church and civic-sponsored "bake sales" to sample some of the local-made baked goods this Saturday morning. Eventually, we got down to business and set out westward at 11:00 for the long day's ride.

Cycling is like a church — many attend, but few understand. — **Jim Burlant**

John and Jeff preparing for departure. This is the main intersection of town. The building behind is the DeTour Express Market, where the three of us enjoyed our "post-play dinner" the night before.

The first leg of our day's ride took us down Hwy 134, which parallels the scenic northern shore of Lake Huron. The next four pages depict some of the great vistas along this route.

Highway 134 winds along the forest edge, with Lake Huron on the south side.

The northern shore of Lake Huron is picturesquely curvy and affords many great photo opportunities.

A shoreline of conifers, field plants, and limestone rock.

One of many little bays along Lake Huron's northern shore.

B331

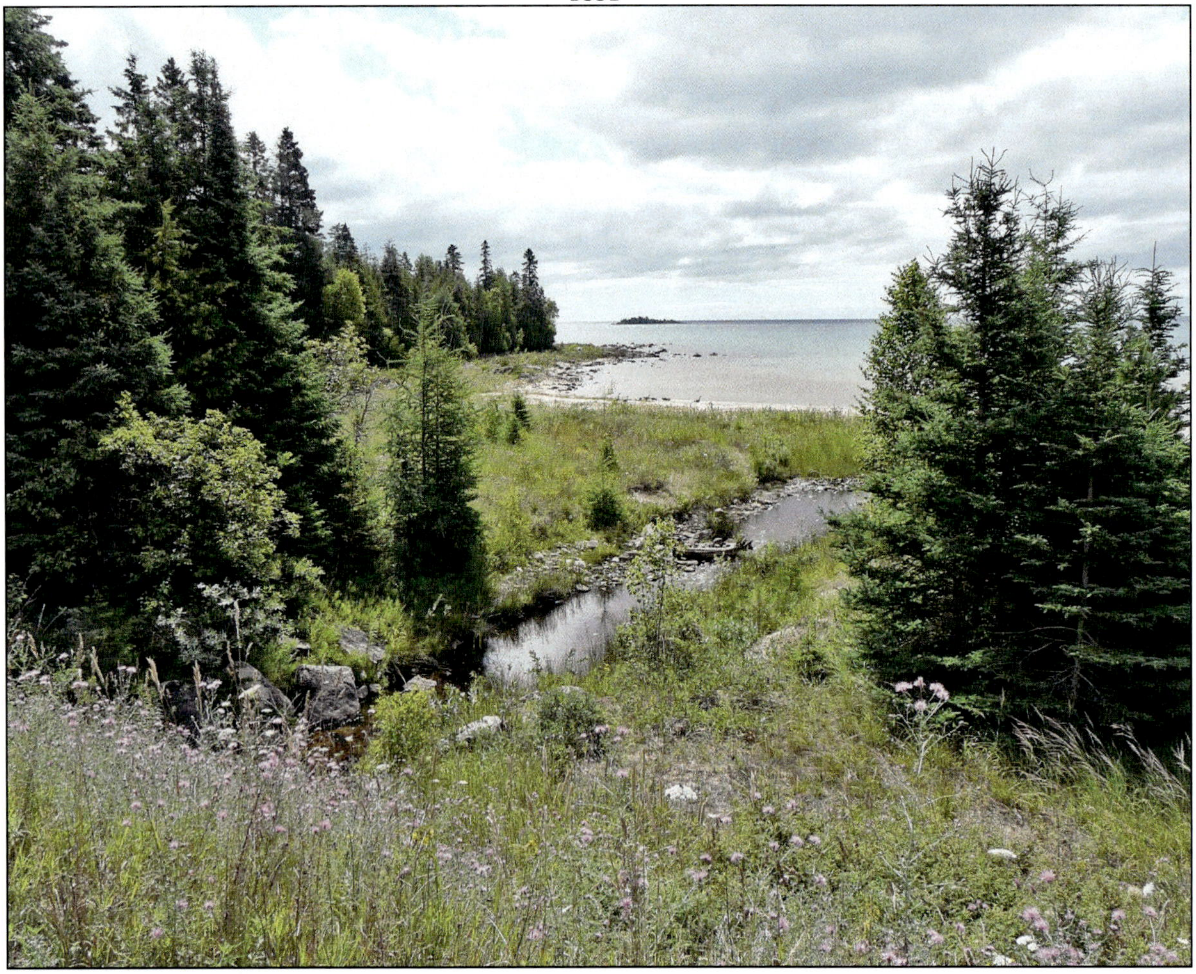

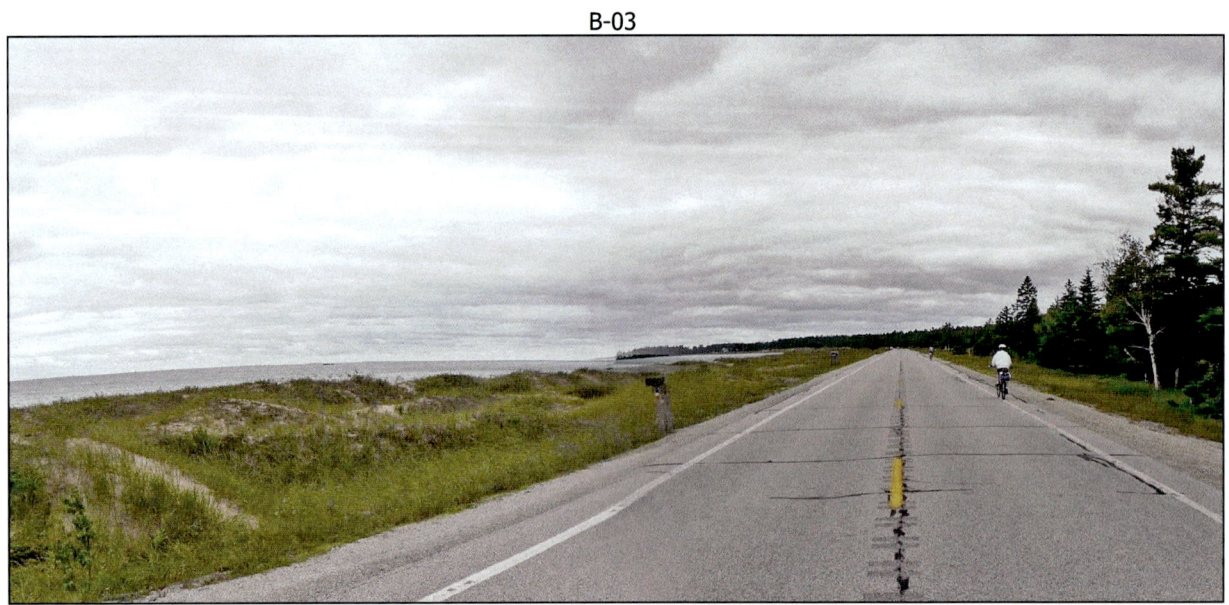

The Lake Huron northern shoreline comprises numerous coves, inlets, shallow rocky flats, and islands.

B-03

In the morning we had sun. Later, expansive cloud cover took over.

An impressive limestone processing facility. Limestone abounds in this region of the U.P., due to the geological formation known as the Niagara Escarpment.

Jeff first, Bill second (John third).
Jeff enjoyed being the lead rider, and Bill often took second position, so this was a frequent view of mine on the first two days of the tour as Jeff accompanied us. (Side note: Being "third man" isn't bad. It provides extra entertainment.)

Day 2 | DeTour to Trout Lake

At one point we stopped to answer nature's call. At which time Bill and Jeff discovered thimbleberries, and proceeded to pick a few for eating.

Sandhill cranes, commonly called "sandhills," are an impressive bird and a common sight in the Upper Peninsula in summer (they migrate south for winter). Small groups frequently can be spotted along the roadside.

A family of sandhills crossing the curvy highway.

As we approached the town of Cedarville we came upon the Les Cheneaux Maritime Museum. Our nautical instincts compelled us to check it out.

It's a most interesting place, especially if you're into classical boats and Great Lakes nautical history.
For info on the museum, visit: lchistorical.org

Following are photos taken inside the museum.

Jeff and Bill discussing weighty nautical matters. (Or, perhaps Jeff is showing the length of his last fish.)

John with a classic 1950s 16-foot Lyman boat (under restoration).
This is the exact same model of boat that John's father purchased in 1956, and which he kept until 2005 when it was given to a wooden boat restorer. In the 1950s and '60s clinker-constructed Lymans were a popular watercraft, especially in the Great Lakes region. But manufacture ceased long ago, as fiberglass and aluminum replaced wood.

Bill admiring the artistry of an under-construction handmade wooden canoe — a Wee Lassie — which he discovered in a workshop in the museum. Bill found it especially interesting, as he has pursued wooden boat-building for years as a hobby.

SIDE NOTE: Also in Cedarville is the impressive Great Lakes Boat Building School. On our 2009 bike tour Bill and I stopped there and received an inspiring guided tour of the facility by veteran boat craftsman Paul Wilson.

Bill, Paul Wilson, John — Great Lakes Boat Building School, Cedarville, MI —
a school dedicated to "the art and craft of traditional and contemporary wooden boat building."
Paul, by the way, is the head boat-builder on the Wee Lassie (C23, prior page). For info on the school: www.glbbs.org.

After departing the maritime museum we continued on toward Hessel, our lunch stop. Along this stretch we passed a "fellow cross-country cyclist."

Except for a trio of three bikers we met on Day 3 at our motel, this guy is the only cross-country cyclist we encountered during our entire week on the road.

Unique ice cream stand on Hwy 124 near Hessel.

Each year the Les Cheneaux Islands community (a collection of inhabited islands in Lake Huron near Hessel) sponsors an impressive antique wooden boat show around the first or second weekend in August. It features a flotilla of impressive classic watercraft, some of which come from as far away as Florida and California.

If you like boats, especially restored classic boats, you'd love attending this event.
(Unfortunately, we arrived here one weekend too soon.)
For info on future shows — www.lchistorical.org

The Hessel Grocery Market — our Saturday lunch stop. (We also ate here on our 2009 tour.)

Enjoying lunch inside the Hessel Market —
John with a tuna salad sub and Jeff with "the most memorable BLT he's ever had."

After lunch we hit the highway with renewed determination (which we needed for biking into a relentless headwind). But, about a quarter mile down the road we came upon the Hessel Home Bakery. Well, of course, that made us realize we had overlooked perhaps the most essential lunch component of all — *dessert*. So we stopped to get some sweet treats to carry with us. As we approached the door we noticed the store hours sign: "Open 7 a.m. to 3 p.m." It was now 3:10. But I pulled on the door anyhow and it opened. Inside were a pair of women busily cleaning up. They appeared to be a mother/daughter team. One of them said, "Sorry, we're closed." I said, "How about we just get some cookies to go?" "Okay, we can handle that," she replied. So we each selected from their impressive cookie display, and requested they pack them into plastic bags for us, which they did (they used plastic bread bags for it).

After getting our vital cookies we readied for departure, once again.
(That "thing" in the lower left corner — it's Bill's bag of "tasty cookies for the road." Bill often likes to include some "foreground" in his photos. For this photo his cookies got the honor.)

I found the bakery's front roof sign compelling: *"The best!* pasties in the north." How bold is that! Had I seen it before lunch I might have been enticed to put it to the test. Perhaps we'll do it the next time we come down this route ... if we ever do it again. Oh, one last thing: the cookies of the Hessel Home Bakery — they were great! Check them out if you're ever in the area.

During the entire week Bill was on the lookout for unique photo ops. And, he's not hesitant about trying something different. Here's one of those "different" shots.

B349

(The bird's not really dead; it's just so mortified from being in a photo like this it fainted.)

C30

I took this photo of Bill while he was preparing to take the above photo (B349). Just as I was about to snap it a car with a young woman stopped beside me. She rolled down the passenger window and, somewhat frantically, said, "Is everything all right, do you need me to go for help?" I said "He's just setting up to take a picture of a dead bird." She laughed, shook her head, and drove away.

At the point were Hwy 134 crosses over expressway I-75 we encountered a produce stand tucked into a space at the southeast corner of the junction. We decided to stop for something to eat. Behind the stand, nestled in the trees as if to hide it, was an RV trailer and one of those outside porta-potties. We stopped at this stand on our 2009 tour as well. But at that time it comprised a canvas canopy, as opposed to a permanent structure, and didn't have as much stock. So this side-of-the-road business has apparently thrived over the years.

Bill sinking his chompers into a juicy peach — which cost $1.00 each!

Eat before you are hungry. Drink before you are thirsty. Rest before you are tired. Cover up before you are cold. Peel off before you are hot. Don't drink or smoke on tour. Never ride just to prove yourself. — **Paul de Vivie, a.k.a. Velocio**

A couple hundred yards after crossing over I-75 we came to road H63, known as Mackinac Trail. We rode southward on Mackinac Trail for eight miles. Those eight miles were the only stretch of the 74-mile ride that day that wouldn't involve a headwind. Along the way we crossed the Carp River (known for its trout and salmon fishing, not carp fishing) and came upon the Carp River Campground, which is in Hiawatha National Forest. We took a 10-minute side excursion into the campground, to check it out.

Eventually H63 intersected Hwy 123. It was now around 6:00 o'clock. We turned onto 123 and rode northwest toward Trout Lake for the final leg of the day's ride. This leg was about 20 miles long and involved a direct assault into the wind, which also happened to be the strongest wind of the day as it had been gaining velocity as the hours progressed. Plus, the temperature had been getting colder after 4:00 p.m. and had now turned chilly. When we reached the town of Moran, which comprises a couple small businesses and a few homes, we stopped at a gas station to "use the facilities" and get a bite of food.

By the time we had reached Moran, which was around 6:30, the constant grind of peddling into brother wind had taken its toll not only on our legs but on our mental disposition as well. We were no longer riding with an eye for photo ops. And, were no longer chatting and joking. Instead, we were into a "silent, head down, nose to the road, how many more darn miles are left to go?" frame of mind. Eventually we arrived at the tiny town of Trout Lake and our lodging facility for the night, McGowan's Motel. It was just a few minutes before 8:00 p.m.

McGowan's Motel & Restaurant — on the right side of the tracks.
(It looked the same in 2013 as it did in 2009.)

As previously arranged, Bill's wife Pam was there to drive Jeff and his bike back to the Soo that evening. So Bill and I checked into our motel room and changed into street clothes. Then the four of us walked across the parking lot to the motel restaurant for dinner. We entered the restaurant at 8:03 and sat down at a table. But the waitress informed us that they closed at

8:00 and, so, couldn't serve us. So we did a 50-yard stroll down the block (the entire business district of the town is about a block long) to the Buckhorn Inn, one of two taverns in town.

The Buckhorn Inn — our dinner spot in Trout Lake.
(This is how it looked in 2009. It looked the same in 2013, except Frank's portion of the front signage was now gone.)

John, Pam, Jeff waiting for dinner at the Buckhorn. After dinner the four of us walked to the local IGA grocery/general store (about 50 yards down the block) and each ordered an ice cream cone for dessert. Shortly after that Pam and Jeff departed for the Soo and Bill and I hit the sack for a welcomed night's sleep.

John recording day's events in his notebook, while at the Buckhorn Inn.
(I recorded notes each day for the writing of this book. Bill and I usually did this at dinner time.)

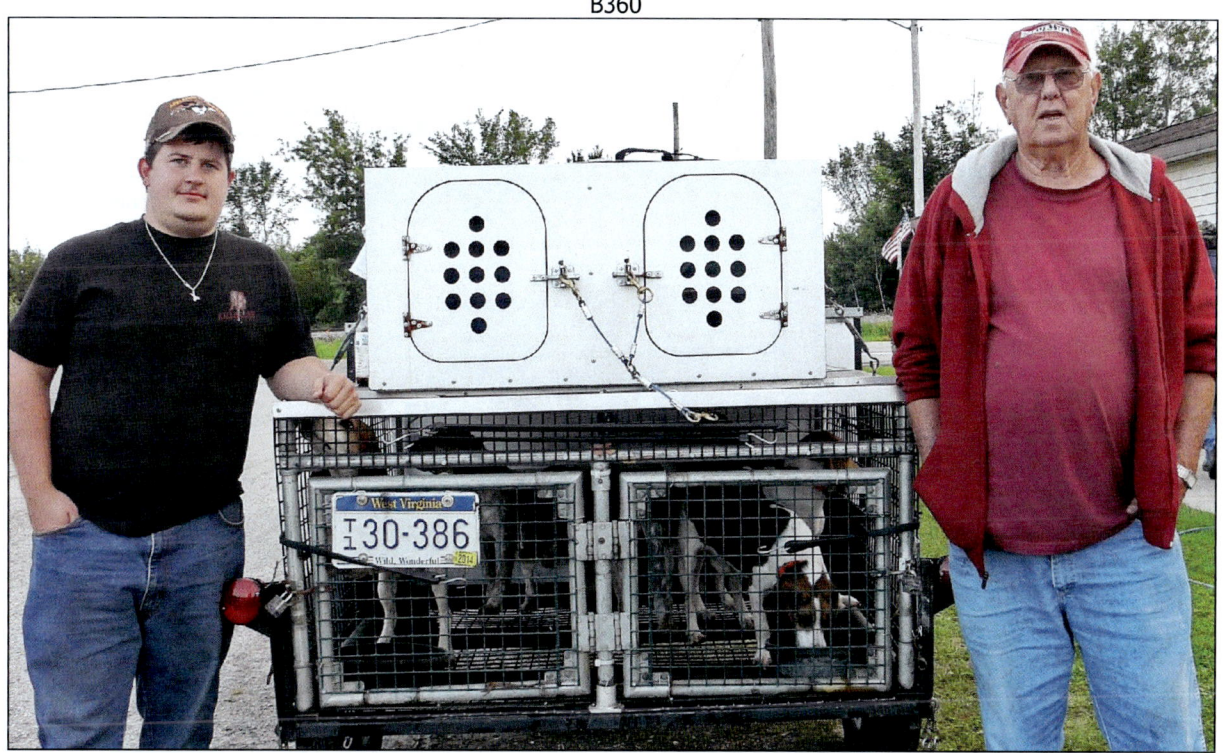

At the same time we arrived at McGowan's two trailer loads of beagles had also arrived.
They were a father/son team from West Virginia and Ohio. Hunting season wasn't yet open but they were there to prepare their hounds for rabbit hunting by chasing U.P. snowshoe hares. When Bill and I were in Trout Lake in 2009 these *same* gentlemen and their dogs were also staying at McGowan's at that time.

Day 2 | DeTour to Trout Lake

~ Day 3 ~
Trout Lake to Blaney Park

DATE: Sunday, August 4, 2013

LUNCH STOP: None — carried food with us

ROUTE: H40 (called Hiawatha Trail) west to Hwy 117 (in Engadine) — Hwy 117 south to U.S. 2 — U.S. 2 west to Dreamland Motel

LODGING: Dreamland Motel — it's located on U.S. 2 about two miles west of Hwy 77 — the mailing address of the motel is Gulliver, but it's closer to Blaney Park

TOTAL MILES: 52

Bill and I arose that morning around 7:30, dressed, and walked across the motel parking lot to the motel restaurant for breakfast. On our way we noticed three BMW motorcycles in front of the room next to ours. There were other motorcycles in the lot beside these three, but they were all Harleys or Harley look-alikes, which made the three BMWs stand out. During breakfast three elderly men strolled into the restaurant and sat down. Bill said to me, "I bet those are the three BMW riders." As it turned out, they were.

Three gentlemen BMW riders at McGowan's.

So we struck up a conversation with them and found out they were three friends, two who lived in southern Michigan and the other in Ohio. All three were retired and they were returning from a Montana trip. They said they'd been traveling 300 to 400 miles a day, and sometimes up to 600.

•

Most people view a bike tour as merely peddling a long distance. But it's actually way more than that. It's everything you experience between the starting peddle stroke and when you jump off the saddle for the last time at the end.

On our 2009 tour we ate lunch on Day 3 in Engadine at a neat little restaurant/bakery called Mary's Garden, Bakery & Café. But in 2009 we were traveling through Engadine on Monday; this time it would be Sunday. So we assumed that Mary's Café might be closed. This being the case, we decided to carry lunch with us, which meant we needed to get some food before leaving Trout Lake. So after breakfast we walked to the IGA grocery store at the north end of town by the railroad track (about a 200-yard walk from our motel), and procured some food items for carrying with us, and then walked back to our motel room and proceeded to get ready for departure.

Typically, when Bill and I get ready in the morning it takes Bill only a few minutes while I spend more time. So, after Bill does his preparations he usually lays down and relaxes while waiting for me to finish. This morning, however, he didn't lay down but, instead, just kept futzing around with packing as I was getting ready. I didn't take notice of this change of routine at the time, until Bill broke the silence with a startling statement: "John, have you seen my wallet?"

"Oooh no," I thought to myself. I asked him if he had checked his bag. Yes, he had emptied it. I asked if he had looked everywhere. Yes, everyplace he could think of. So the two of us looked "everyplace we could think of" again. Still, no wallet. The only place left that we hadn't checked was my bag. So I unpacked my bag to make sure I hadn't somehow packed it between some pieces of dirty clothing. No wallet.

Bill then said, "I'm going to ride down to the IGA market and see if I might have left it on the counter." He jumped on his bike and took off. In a few minutes he returned, "The clerk and I walked the entire store and couldn't find it."

I then said, "We need to trace our *exact* steps from when we left the restaurant and walked down to the market, and then around the market, and back to our room." So we began by walking from our motel room across the motel parking lot to the front sidewalk, and then down the sidewalk toward the market. And, of course, as we did we kept looking left and right for a wallet. With each step the chances of finding it appeared less and less.

Then, just before we reached the IGA by the railroad track, we encountered a joyous sight.

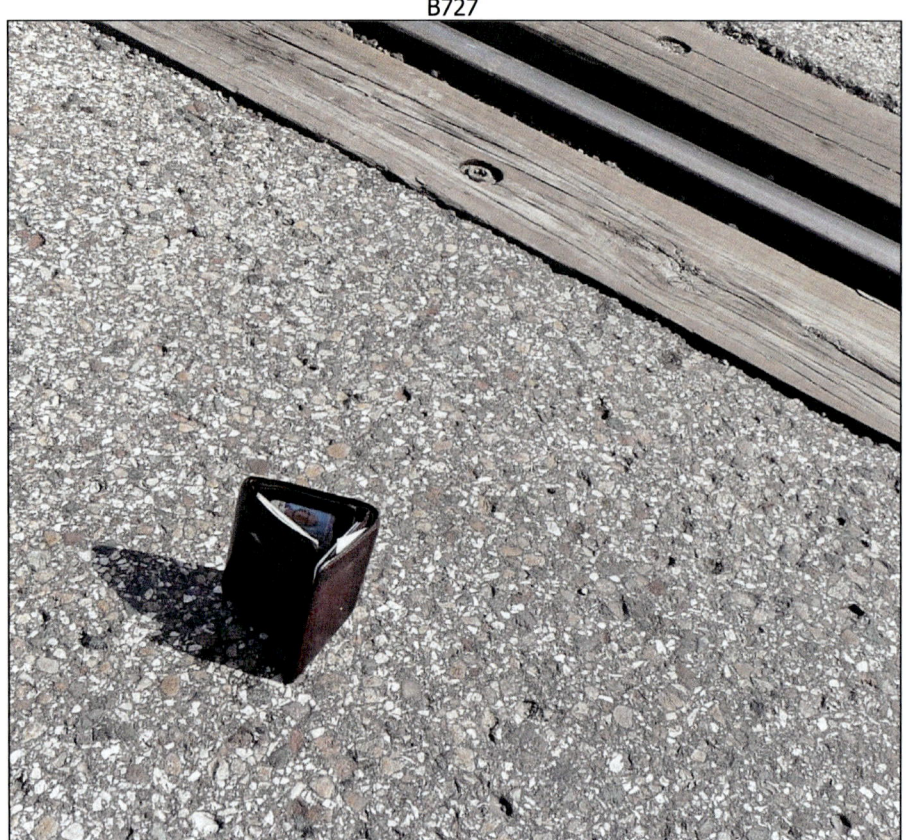

Sitting coyly on the sidewalk beside the railroad track is Bill's wallet.
(No, this isn't a photo taken at the moment we found the wallet, but a photographic reproduction of what we saw.)

Needless to say, finding the wallet *made our day*. So what happened? Apparently, when Bill slid his wallet into his back pocket (in the IGA store), it had not totally slid into the pocket and, so, fell out as we were walking back to the motel.

•

Our longest, hardest day of the tour was the previous day (Day 2); today would be one of our easiest: only 52 miles. We did have a headwind this day, as in the prior day, but not nearly as strong. Because of the wallet incident we departed Trout Lake around 11:00 a.m. The first leg of the ride took us westward on highway H40, or Hiawatha Trail. Traffic was minimal and the ride most enjoyable. On the next few pages are photos we took along the way (for convenience we've also included a few pics taken on our 2009 trip along this same route).

SIDE NOTE: A common structure in Michigan's Upper Peninsula is a certain form of residential architecture. It comprises a mobile home with a free-standing roof built over it. This is probably to eliminate heavy snow weight on the house and also prevent any chance of roof leaks. Some of these "super-roof" structures are quite elaborate, with carports and porch roofs included. Many have a metal top covering, as opposed to shingles. Forest green seems to be the preferred color — quite attractive — as illustrated in this photo (P38 next page).

One of the many uniquely charming country abodes of the U.P.

Along this route we came upon an alpaca ranch guarded by a pair of Giant Pyrenees dogs.

Two Giant Pyrenees livestock guard dogs protecting a herd of alpacas.
Wolf packs have been gradually spreading eastward from Wisconsin into Michigan's U.P. Generally, wolves will kill and eat anything on four legs, except for bears *and* perhaps Giant Pyrenees. To protect livestock, this alpaca ranch has two perimeters of fencing enclosing the herd. The dogs patrol the area between the two fences. They ignored us, until Bill began walking up to the fence for a photo. They then ran out and firmly told him, "Stop there."

B370

On the road to Rexton.
You'll note that in most of the 2009 photos Bill and I are in short sleeves. But in many of the 2013 photos (like above) we're wearing a long-sleeve shirt and sometimes a jacket, too. The weather was slightly cooler than usual on the 2013 tour — most days a high in the upper 60s, or at least starting in the 60s and progressing only to the low 70s. So we ended up wearing our "emergency" long-sleeve shirts much of the time.

Eventually we came to the town of Rexton, which holds a two-pump gas station with convenience store. We stopped there in 2009 and decided to stop again and eat some lunch (they have a thoughtful picnic table outside the store for folks to eat at).

B372

Snowmobiling is a popular winter sport and tourist attraction in the U.P. So snowmobile trails abound.
There happens to be one such trail running beside the gas station in Rexton. It crosses the road in front of the station. Note the billboard advertising (by Johnny B's Pub) aimed at snowmobilers. It even includes a thoughtful map (right side of billboard).

Day 3 | Trout Lake to Blaney Park

Snowmobile stop sign and directions.
This sign post, adjacent the Rexton gas station, is located where the snowmobile trail crosses the road.
The bottom sign tells us that Trout Lake is "12 miles that way."

After lunch at the gas station we continued westward on Hiawatha Trail toward the town of Engadine. Following are photos taken on the way.

A coil of fiber optic cable.
Along the roadside in this area of the U.P. we kept seeing installation diggings for
fiber optic cable — so super-fast Internet connection must be soon coming to the northland.

An Outdoorsman's Garage — it's a *real* garage, a *Yooper* garage.
Being attuned to outdoor life, Yoopers tend to go for he-man size garages, as opposed to those little, sissy car-only structures of the big-city burbs. It caused Bill to whimsically quip, "Did you know, there's a zoning ordinance in the U.P. that your garage must be bigger than your house."

Bill and John (l-and-r) on the Hiawatha Trail, heading westward to Engadine.

Yup, sandhill cranes again — must be mama, papa, and junior or little missy (trailing behind)

Eventually, we arrived at the pleasant little crossroads town of Engadine.

Mary's Garden, Bakery & Café — 2009. On our 2009 tour we had lunch at Mary's — really great food. Back then the "Open" sign beckoned us. So we had hoped that perhaps Mary's would be open this Sunday and we could eat there again. But the "Open" sign out front had been replaced by a paper taped to the front door: "Closed until further notice." Bill and I were truly sadden; our 2009 lunch there was, indeed, memorable.

This main intersection of town comprises a tavern on one corner, a small IGA market on another, and Mary's Garden, Bakery & Café on a third corner. As Bill and I started to ride away a woman came from the IGA. I asked her what happened to Mary's. She replied, "When we ask her she says 'I can't tell you now.' So I guess it must be a big secret." Then she turned and walked into the tavern.

Bill and I rode a couple miles down the road to where it intersects U.S. 2. Then we turned westward for the last leg of the day's ride. This section of highway contains numerous reminders of yesteryear. One of them is the type of motel that popped up after World War II, when Americans began to "take to the road." Instead of being a single building these lodgings comprised a cluster of little quaint cottages. On our 2009 tour Bill and I took photos of some of them (like this one below). But, sadly, we noticed on our 2013 tour that some of them had closed, and that some that were still open appeared worse for the wear.

Motels comprising individual cottages — a reminder of yesteryear, but are beginning to fade away.

This photo shows Highway U.S. 2 where it crosses a railroad track. Although we're a long way from home, this track winds its way to Engadine, Trout Lake, and eventually to Sault Ste Marie, and goes within a quarter mile of Bill's place.

Our "Home Sweet Home" on August 4, 2013.

We arrived at the Dreamland Motel around 6:00 p.m. As we pulled into the driveway Bill exclaimed, "Hey look, there's some other bikers here." Parked in front of the motel were three touring bicycles with saddle bags, and sitting at a picnic table out front were three bikers — two women and one man — still in their biking attire.

Bill and I pulled up to the entrance door of the restaurant and parked our bikes. (At this motel and also at McGowan's at Trout Lake, the cashier's counter in the restaurant doubles as the "registration desk" for the motel.) As we rode up, the folks at the picnic table took note of us. Then the man jumped up, a beer bottle in hand, and shouted to us. And then, with a welcoming smile, he walked over to us

"Hey, guess what," he said enthusiastically, "you can get a beer and have it put on your room tab, here. When you get checked in, grab a drink and come over and sit with us." So Bill and I did just that. We promptly got our room key, took our bikes to our room, went back and got a beer from the restaurant, and then walked over to the picnic table to meet our new "friends from the road." (Side note: As I was pushing my bike into the room I noticed a slight feeling of "mushiness" as it rolled across the carpeting. I concluded that this meant the carpet had an extra-cushy pad underneath.)

As Bill and I approached the picnic table the three bikers eagerly greeted us and immediately introduced themselves — Anne, Ben, and Jennifer. "Judging from your bikes," I said, "it appears that you're traveling a farther distance than we are." All three nodded and smiled. It was that type of smile that says, "Oh, yes, we are traveling a *very* long distance."

Day 3 | Trout Lake to Blaney Park

(l-to-r) Jennifer, Anne, Ben, John — discussing biking routes, referring to a map of the U.P.

Later, Ben, Jennifer, and Anne prepared a tasty supper, campground style. From the appearance and aroma, it appeared to be some form of chicken/vegetable stew. At the time of this photo it's now about 7:30 p.m. and the temperature was dropping, hence the jackets and caps. The two bikes at the motel (behind) are Ben's and Anne's. Bill took this photo as we were walking to the restaurant for supper. They had picked up their "dinner fixins" in a market about ten miles farther back. At that time they weren't aware that the Dreamland Motel also included a restaurant.

Prior to dinner, Bill and I sat and chatted with these folks for about three-quarters of an hour. The conversation flowed freely, as if we were old friends who had just met after a long absence. And, it also was informative and stimulating. We looked at maps and talked about where we'd been so far and where we were heading. These three were truly interesting. Here's their story (as best I recall it).

Ben and Anne are married and live in Tennessee. Jennifer is their friend and lives in Washington State. Ben is a retired oncologist, Anne a retired physical therapist, and Jennifer an HR exec between jobs. If I were to make a guess at their ages, I'd say that Ben is in his 60s, Anne in her 50s, and Jennifer in her 30s. They were in the process of doing a coast-to-coast bike tour across the United States. They had departed from Washington around June first and were heading to Maine and planned to arrive there mid-September, although they were considering adding an extension to the trip, which would result in them ultimately ending up in Virginia.

To get themselves and their bikes from Tennessee to Washington, Anne and Ben took the rails. They said the train ride was great, one of the most enjoyable trips they've been on. Since departing Washington the trio had biked through both the Cascades and the Rockies. I asked them what it was like — was it hard climbing the Rockies? Ben then said, "Do you have three gears on your crankset, including a super-low granny gear?" I told him yes. "Well," he continued, "you just put your bike in its lowest gear and grind away. You could do it."

Their journey also took them through Montana. "At one point," Jennifer explained, "we didn't see a car for *ten miles* — we had it all to ourselves." (Wow, ten miles, that's almost an hour of car-free, total solitude touring — just you, the wind, and the highway — very cool!) They also took a "side-trip" to Denver (on bikes), where they spent a week with some family of Ben and Anne. There, Ben bought a new bike seat from a bike shop. He got what many regard as the best, most comfortable seat on the market: a leather Brooks Imperial.

They were each carrying about 40 pounds of gear, most of it stashed into four pannier bags, a.k.a. saddle bags. (Forty pounds of gear may not sound like much to be carrying on a bike, but believe me it is. I was carrying 30 pounds and it felt plenty heavy.) About two-thirds of the time they did tent-camping in campgrounds, and the other third they stayed at motels. Their ride on this particular day was from Escanaba to the Dreamland Motel (via U.S. 2). They hadn't realized that the motel had a restaurant. So they stopped in Manistique and got dinner fixings. That's why they "cooked out" in front of the Dreamland restaurant that evening (photo B395).

Their next day's ride would take them to St. Ignace. After that they would cross the Bridge, spend a day doing sightseeing in Mackinaw City and Mackinac Island. Then they would wind their way across the Lower Peninsula to Marine City on the St. Clair River, take the ferry across to Canada, ride through Ontario to Niagara, and then back into the States and eastward to Maine. (Actually, I'm not certain Niagara was their re-entry point back into the States.)

Bill and I also described our 7-day Michigan U.P. tour (which, of course, paled in comparison to what they were doing), but they still were interested in hearing of it.

We also took the opportunity to tap into their technical knowledge of cross-country bike touring. We asked questions, they supplied answers — and informative ones, too. Of particular interest to us was what they used for rain attire, and for biking shoes, and types of pedals, and types of tires, and what types of bikes they were riding. At one point Anne took Bill and me over to her and Ben's bikes (parked in front of their room). She pointed out what makes a touring bike different from a road bike.

At this time I noticed the Brooks saddle on Ben's bike. I've read that it takes some time to "break in" a Brooks so that the leather seat conforms to the contour of your bottom and, thereby, makes for its legendary comfortable ride. However, this saddle on Ben's bike was a flat surface front to rear — no trace of any contour from a biker's bottom. Out of curiosity I pushed down on it with my fingers to see how "firm" it was; it was *very* firm. The leather surface seemed unyielding. Then Anne chuckled and said, "Ben bought this Brooks saddle when we were in Denver. The bike store salesman told him it would take about a hundred miles of riding to break it in. Well, Ben has been on it for over a thousand miles now, and instead of Ben breaking in the saddle, the saddle is breaking in Ben." Bill and I laughed. But I did, indeed, feel sympathy for Ben.

Pretty soon we all had to get ready for dinner. Bill and I needed to shower and don street clothes and they had to start cooking. Shortly after I got into the motel room I moved my bike a few feet. At that point I got the shocker: my rear tire was totally flat! (I then realized why the carpeting felt cushy when I first entered the room; my rear tire was partially flat at the time.) I ran my hand around the deflated tire and discovered an industrial staple. I marked the spot on the tire, pulled out the staple, laid the bike on its side, and proceeded to repair the puncture. It didn't take long to get the hole patched and the tire remounted. But pumping up the tire to 50 psi with a dinky travel pump took some effort, which Bill thoughtfully assisted with.

John applying a patch to the puncture in his new "puncture-proof" tire.

About three weeks prior, in preparation for the tour, I had taken my bike to a local bike shop and had them replace the rear tire. I told the owner I wanted the most puncture-resistant tire he had. He said, "That's the Specialized Armadillo. You definitely won't get a flat with that one." I said, "Great, that's the one I want." Well, one pesky little staple was all it took to bring the vaunted Armadillo to its knees. Fortunately for me, the patch job "held." (The Armadillo is still on my bike, two months later, fully pumped up, and the tube is non-leaking.)

By the time we finished with everything it was getting close to eight o'clock, which was when the restaurant closed. So Bill and I hustled on over to eat. The restaurant was featuring a baked chicken dinner that evening, which we both enjoyed. Soon afterward we called it a day, got into our beds, and then discovered a Tigers baseball game on TV. We watched some of it, and fell asleep before it ended.

You get a feeling on certain trails, when you're reacting like you and your machine are just one thing. It's the feeling of physical exertion and speed and technique all wrapped into one.
*— **Ned Overend***

*Melancholy is incompatible with bicycling. — **James E. Starrs***

*The best rides are the ones where you bite off much more than you can chew — and live through it. — **Doug Bradbury***

When man invented the bicycle he reached the peak of his attainments. Here was a machine of precision and balance for the convenience of man. And (unlike subsequent inventions for man's convenience) the more he used it, the fitter his body became. Here, for once, was a product of man's brain that was entirely beneficial to those who used it, and of no harm or irritation to others. Progress should have stopped when man invented the bicycle.
*— **Elizabeth West, Hovel in the Hills***

*The bicycle is the perfect transducer to match man's metabolic energy to the impedance of locomotion. Equipped with this tool, man outstrips the efficiency of not only all machines but all other animals as well. — **Ivan Illich, Energy and Equity***

*Let me tell you what I think of bicycling. I think it has done more to emancipate women than anything else in the world. It gives women a feeling of freedom and self-reliance. I stand and rejoice every time I see a woman ride by on a wheel ... the picture of free, untrammeled womanhood. — **Susan B. Anthony***

*A bicycle does get you there and more.... And there is always the thin edge of danger to keep you alert and comfortably apprehensive. Dogs become dogs again and snap at your raincoat; potholes become personal. And getting there is all the fun. — **Bill Emerson, "On Bicycling," Saturday Evening Post, July 1967***

~ Day 4 ~
Blaney Park to Munising

DATE: Monday, August 5, 2013

LUNCH STOP: Jack Pine Lodge (on Hwy 94 near Steuban)

ROUTE: U.S. 2 west to Hwy 94 (in Manistique) — Hwy 94 north to Hwy 28 — Hwy 28 west to Munising

LODGING: Munising Motel (in Munising)

TOTAL MILES: 66

The prior evening's TV weather forecast predicted rain for this afternoon. So we decided to try to escape the wet stuff by getting an early start this morning and, thereby, perhaps reach Munising before the rain arrived. With that in mind, we had an early breakfast at the Dreamland restaurant, packed, suited up, and got on the road at 8:30 a.m. Following are photos taken "on the road to Manistique."

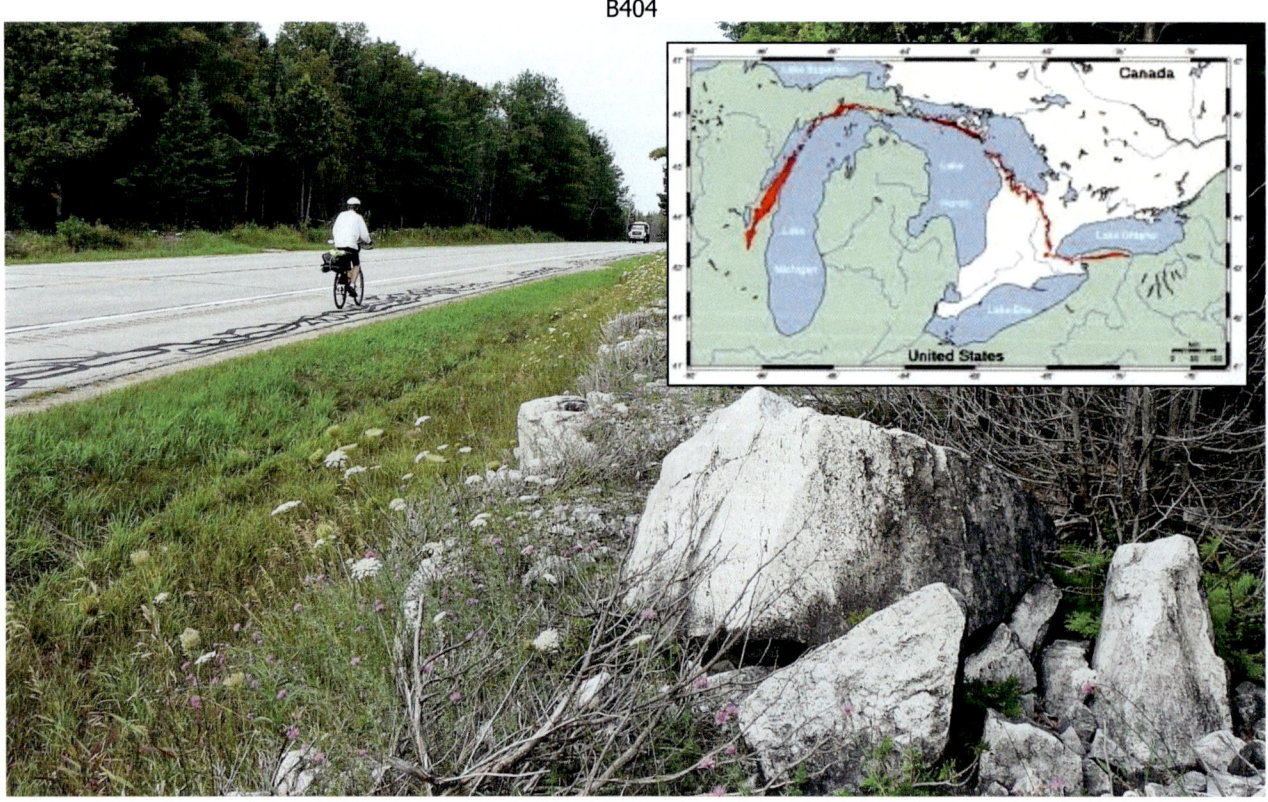

Limestone along the roadside of U.S. 2. We encountered a lot of this on Days 2 and 3.
Limestone outcropping is part of the Niagara Escarpment, which follows the southern shore of the U.P. in this region. The inset map shows the entire Escarpment (in red), which forms Niagara Falls near the east end.

Soon we came to an interesting-looking produce/greenhouse/landscape business — The Farm Greenhouse. Bill, an avid gardener, suggested we stop. The creative front signage tickled our photographic fancy.

Bill "mixing it up" with Bigfoot at The Farm Greenhouse.
We each got an apple from the Farm Greenhouse, which Bill is eating while "chatting" with Bigfoot. Also, the gracious owners allowed us to use their bathroom facilities — a gesture we much appreciated.

Bill pondering an interesting vista where U.S. 2 crosses over a railroad track.

The prior evening we had gotten into a brief discussion on the subject of bike tires with the coast-to-coast trio. I mentioned I was riding on 2-inch tires. This prompted one of them to ask "how much pressure are you running with them?"

I responded, "About fifty pounds." They then said, "What's the max you can put in?" I said, "Sixty five." To which they replied, "So why aren't you running at sixty five?" After that I decided I should go with max pressure, to make for easiest-possible peddling.

So eventually Bill and I came upon a gas station. We turned in to "top off" the pressure in our tires with the station's air hose. I pumped up both of mine to 65 psi. Bill attempted to pump his up to 100, but he could go only as high as 90, as the gas station's air compressor was incapable of going higher than that. (And, yes, the extra 15 pounds of air pressure in my tires did make for easier peddling; something I greatly appreciated.)

Pretty soon we were closing in on Manistique. About five miles from town, small businesses and motels began to appear. At about two miles from town U.S. 2 comes close to the Lake Michigan shore and runs parallel to it, with only about a hundred yards between the lake and roadway. In the area between lake and roadway there's a two-mile long walking path that extends into Manistique. And, between the path and water there's an attractive natural shoreline. This photo depicts the natural beauty of the Lake Michigan shore along this area.

P59(2009)

The walking path begins in Manistique and runs eastward for a couple miles between the roadway and lake.
(In this photo the path is to the right.)

The western terminus of the path is about a block from downtown Manistique. It's near a walkway that goes out to the Manistique Lighthouse, officially named Manistique East Breakwater Light. Here's a photo showing it (P61 next page).

One can walk out to the lighthouse (it's actually a bit trickier and scarier than it appears in this photo).

Manistique is located on the north shore of Lake Michigan where the Manistique River empties into the lake. It's a nifty little town, with the upside of a larger city but none of the downside. It has a small town feel, and contains only one traffic light, as best I recollect. Yet, it has a harbor, marina, a number of nice motels, the previously mentioned walking path, and an assortment of restaurants and taverns. The business district is viable and beckoning, but not overwhelming, and includes both traditional names and newer ones. And, outside the city are a couple small shopping centers anchored by a larger chain store. (For more info on Manistique, visit www.cityofmanistique.org)

It is curious that with the advent of the automobile and the airplane, the bicycle is still with us. Perhaps people like the world they can see from a bike, or the air they breathe when they're out on a bike. Or they like the bicycle's simplicity and precision with which it is made. Or because they like the feeling of being able to hurtle through air one minute, and saunter through a park the next, without leaving behind clouds of choking exhaust, without leaving behind so much as a footstep. — **Gurdon S. Leete**

The bicycle is the most civilized conveyance known to man. Other forms of transport grow daily more nightmarish. Only the bicycle remains pure in heart. — **Iris Murdoch, The Red and the Green**

From U.S. 2 we turned north into the small but charming business district of the city and crossed the bridge spanning the Manistique River.

The unique Manistique water tower, located next to the main bridge that crosses the Manistique River.

After crossing this bridge we came to Hwy 94 and took it northbound out of town. We stayed on this road for the next 35 miles, until it intersected Hwy 28 in Shingleton. The wind this day came from the south. We were biking mostly northward. So, for the first time since Day 1 we had a backwind. We enjoyed it immensely. Combined with the sunny blue sky that we had for the next couple hours it made for beautiful cycling. On the next several pages are photos of things we encountered along this route.

Northbound on Hwy 94, we had sunny sky for the first hour and backwind or sidewind all the way.
Hwy 94 comprises good road, light traffic, and abundant wilderness — perfect for idyllic biking.

After about an hour we came to Hiawatha. On most maps Hiawatha shows as a decent-sized town. But, as far as we could tell, it appeared to constitute only a few houses and a church. The church, albeit small, is quite distinctive. Here's a photo we took of it on our 2009 tour.

**It looked the same in 2013 as it did in 2009, except for one thing:
the bold red cross over the door was no longer there. We wondered why.**

Eventually the sunny blue sky gave way to a broad expanse of grey cloud creeping in from the west. It appeared that the weather forecast for afternoon rain was going to bear out.

Pretty soon we came to the Jack Pine Lodge, our planned lunch stop. We first "stumbled" upon this place on our 2009 tour. Then it was a hot, sunny day. So we had stopped to quench our thirst. But on this afternoon in 2013 the weather was the opposite: grey and cool. So this time we went in for a hot meal.

**The Jack Pine Lodge, an oasis on Hwy 94.
In 2013 it looked virtually identical to what it looked like in 2009.**

The Jack Pine Lodge is located in Hiawatha National Forest. The first version of it was erected in the 1930s (no one knows the exact date or builder), and, as we discovered, has long been legendary in the region, especially with outdoor-sports-minded visitors to the U.P. True to its namesake, the building and most of the interior furniture and furnishings, including bar, tables, and chairs, appear to be built from jack pine trees. Each table base is unique, having been made from a twisted tree stump or root structure. Everything in the place looks like it has had about 25 coats of varnish, which makes it beautiful and gleaming. While it's apparently a gathering place year-round, the busiest time, according to the bartender/day manager Ronda, is when the snow flies — during *snowmobile* season.

To illustrate, on the next page is an aerial photo taken during wintertime, which I borrowed from the Lodge's website.

Jack Pine Lodge in winter (image copied from jackpinelodgeup.com)

Snowmobile season at the Jack Pine Lodge on Hwy 94 in the Hiawatha National Forest in Michigan's U.P. It looks like a "whole different place" than on a sunny day in the summertime (as in photo P73).

When we pulled up to the Lodge there was a woman tending to something next to the building. She greeted us with a hearty "welcome" and then escorted us in. Come to find out she was the bartender (and perhaps day manager on duty) at the time. We inquired of her name and she replied "Ronda."

For old times sake we took a seat at the same table we sat at on our 2009 tour. Here's a photo.

P75(2009)

In 2009 it was a hot sunny day when we "discovered" the Jack Pine Lodge on our way northward on Hwy 94. So at the time Bill and I decided to quench our thirst by splitting a beer.
(Note the unique table base, apparently made from the root structure of a jack pine tree.)

Immediately after we sat down Ronda handed us menus. I studied mine for a couple minutes. The hamburger offering looked good, but I had already had enough burger for the week and, so, was seeking something different. I noticed a grilled cheese sandwich tucked into the "sandwiches" section. I considered getting it but then decided that doing so would be risky, because most places just "throw in" a grilled cheese sandwich to pacify the occasional vegetarian and, as a result, usually produce a mediocre one, at best.

Then Ronda came back to the table. Noticing that I was apparently having difficulty making a selection she said, "Would you like a suggestion on what to try?" With relief I replied "Yes."

"Well," she continued, "if you like grilled cheese sandwiches, I would strongly recommend trying ours. It's very, very good. People rave about it. Some folks come here just for that." So, of course, that clinched it — I ordered the grilled cheese.

In short time Ronda returned with our food. Now, I suspect you probably want to know about the grilled cheese sandwich: Had Ronda told me the truth or was she just BS-ing me?" In a nutshell, it was the tastiest, most unique, most satisfying grilled cheese I've ever had. It fulfilled Ronda's hype ... and more. Like every grilled cheese sandwich it had melted cheese inside. But this one contained more than that. It had *lots* of cheese ... *plus* it was packed with other tasty ingredients mixed in with the cheese, which (as best I recollect) included small pieces of diced chicken and veggies. The result: It tasted great.

After finishing lunch Bill took a couple minutes to snap the following three photos. Then we bid adieu to Ronda and got back on the road.

Beautiful Ronda behind the beautiful bar of the beautiful Jack Pine Lodge.

Uniquely candid sign in the foyer to the restrooms.

We asked Ronda if she knew the weather forecast. She switched the big-screen TV to the weather channel. John is pointing to our location in Michigan's U.P. See the little patch of green to the left of his finger? That's the rain we would be riding through in about 30 minutes after this photo was taken.

Day 4 | Blaney Park to Munising

On the stretch of Hwy 94 between the Jack Pine Lodge and Shingleton the road crosses over three branches of a particular creek. The creek is Stutts Creek and the three branches are the South Branch, Middle Branch, and North Branch. On our 2009 tour Bill and I carried fishing rods so we could do some spontaneous angling. We wet our lines in several places along the way, but caught nothing except for one spot: the North Branch of Stutts Creek. At this particular creek, which is more like a small river than a creek, I hooked a little brook trout. Here's a photo of me fishing there, with Bill "overseeing the situation."

I'm fishing from the bridge on Hwy 94 that goes over the North Branch of Stutts Creek. I hooked a small "brookie" about a minute after this photo was taken. In 2013 we stopped here again to reminisce over our "big catch" in '09. The Creek looked somewhat different from what we recollected because the bushes and trees lining the bank had grown larger and were now overhanging the water to a greater extent.

About this time the rain began. It started as an intermittent light sprinkle and slowly progressed to a steady light rain. It lasted for an hour and a half. During this time we reached the small town of Shingleton, which basically comprises a few small businesses gathered around the intersection of Highways 94 and 28. Here we turned westward onto Hwy 28 for the last leg of our ride that day. This stretch of road carried a fair amount of fast traffic and the shoulder was only three feet wide. The cars whizzing by cast perpetual spray upon us. All this conspired to make for a less-than-fully-enjoyable stretch of biking.

SIDE NOTE: If I were to bike this way again I'd probably take a different route from Shingleton to Munising. Instead of taking Hwy 28 I'd take H15 northward from Shingleton to where it intersects highway H58 and then take H58 westward into Munising — much less traffic.

Eventually we came to a special place where we had stopped in 2009 — a business called The Modern Woodsmith.

The Modern Woodsmith on Hwy 28
If you're ever in the market for a very classy, high-quality custom-made door or other wooden household creation, you would do well to talk with these folks (themodernwoodsmith.com).

Out of curiosity, Bill and I stopped at this business on our 2009 tour. We did it because woodworking is one of Bill's hobbies. As we were approaching the building to go in, the proprietor, Tim Flynn, actually greeted us at the door. After a few minutes of discussion Tim offered to give us a guided tour of his workshop. It turned out to be 20 minutes of really interesting stuff, including the story of how and why he created the business.

This time, however, another fellow greeted us as we entered. We asked for Tim. The man told us Tim was out for a couple hours attending to another new business of his: the *Riptide Ride!* Come to find out, it's a speedboat ride for tourists who want to view the famous Pictured Rocks (located on the Lake Superior shore north of Munising). This business bills itself as "the baddest boat in the bay." So, if you'd like to get a classy custom wooden door *or* view the Pictured Rocks from the baddest boat in Munising's South Bay *or* perhaps both, this is something to check out. (Note: If taking a boat tour of the Pictured Rocks from a speedboat isn't your cup of tea, there's at least one other Pictured Rocks boat ride business, which provides a more leisurely cruise-style experience.) For more on Munising, visit www.munising.org

Upon leaving The Modern Woodsmith we only had about five more miles to go. But before reaching downtown Munising, Hwy 28 undergoes a long descent, like 1.4 miles long. The first half of this drop is gradual, but the last half turns steep.

Day 4 | Blaney Park to Munising

Due to the wet road conditions and heavy traffic I told Bill I intended to take the descent slowly, like no faster than 15 mph. So, if he wanted to go full speed I wouldn't be keeping up with him. Bill, being an adventurer, decided to go for the gusto: a full-speed descent. Shortly after the decline began Bill disappeared from sight. I figured I'd probably be meeting him at the motel. After several minutes the bottom of the hill came into view. To my surprise, Bill was standing there next to his bike. When I got to him I stopped, because Bill hadn't remounted his machine.

Then he said, "The scariest thing just happened to me. I hit 37 miles per hour and then my bike began to do this wobbly shake. At first it was just a little bit, and then it grew. I couldn't control it from the handlebars. I thought I was going to crash. Then I squeezed the top tube between my knees and it stopped the shaking. By that point I was at the bottom of the hill and I came to a stop. Boy, was that scary."

We conjectured about the cause. I thought it might pertain to his handlebars and head tube. He figured it was because of the weight and high position of the load he was carrying. Anyhow, for the rest of the tour he didn't go over about 18 miles per hour at any time.

With Bill recomposed, we biked about two more miles and finally came to our night's lodging: the Munising Motel. By this time the rain had stopped. As it turned out, that would be the last rain that we would bike in. We checked into our room, showered, and walked across the street to Sydney's restaurant for dinner. Bill and I treated ourselves to the establishment's "Dinner Buffet" — an impressive culinary spread.

A welcomed sight after 66 miles in the saddle, the last hour and a half of it in rain.
(This photo was taken the next morning, so the sidewalks are now dry.)

~ Day 5 ~
Munising to Grand Marais

DATE: Tuesday, August 6, 2013
LUNCH STOP: None — carried food with us
ROUTE: H58 east (and northeast) to Grand Marais
LODGING: North Shore Lodge (in Grand Marais)
TOTAL MILES: 51

The first four days of our journey we had followed the same route that we took on our 2009 tour. But now, for Days 5 through 7, we would be adventuring into mostly new terrain. We were eagerly looking forward to it, especially this particular day that took us from Munising to Grand Marais. The route was simple: Get on road H58 in Munising and stay on it until we reached Grand Marais. The first two-thirds of this route winds through Lake Superior State Forest, with the last third going through Pictured Rocks National Lakeshore. Before settling on this road I had done some Internet research the prior winter. I discovered that bikers (meaning, motorcyclists) rave about it. They like it because it has minimal traffic, a winding route, and abundant forest and interesting vistas along the way. All of which sounded perfect to Bill and me.

•

When we awoke this morning the rain was gone, but the sky was still cloudy grey, and the temperature slightly cool. One good thing, however, was wind direction. For the entire day it was from the southwest. Which gave us a backwind for the entire day's ride — something we relished. But the weather prediction did contain one element of slight concern: a 20 percent chance of rain forecasted for the afternoon. Our hope was to get to Grand Marais before any wet stuff materialized.

For breakfast we walked a couple blocks to the Dogpatch restaurant (B427 next page). We had eaten there in 2009 and had a good experience and, so, decided to do a rerun. I asked the server if their oatmeal was good. She assured me it was, so I ordered two bowls and enjoyed both.

Life is like riding a bicycle. To keep your balance you must keep moving. — **Albert Einstein**

Bill after his tasty Dogpatch breakfast — with full tummy and ready to hit the highway. This restaurant, by the way, is an interesting concept, well carried out. Food and service were good. Check it out next time you're in Munising.

Butt-shot of John walking back to the motel. The purple banner reads: *Welcome to Munising, the U.P.'s Best Kept Secret.* (Indeed, Munising is a great little town, with some cool attractions. For info, visit www.munising.org)

Day 5 | Munising to Grand Marais

On the way back to the motel I encountered this gentleman on a morning stroll. His name is Jack Witty. His cap, which sported a red plastic poppy, contained embroidery that indicated he was in the Navy during the Vietnam War. Seventy three years old, he's a retired diesel mechanic who once worked at a local mill. Every morning he walks for one-and-a-half to two hours. It was my good fortune to have crossed paths with him this particular morning on August 6, 2013.

One of the friendly motel pooches. It moseyed into our room to wish us "Good morning."

We proceeded to pack up and get ready for riding. The last thing we did was take our loaded bikes downstairs (our room was on the second floor) and prepare to check out. Before doing so we oiled our bike chains on the deck out back. Then for some reason I got this hunch that it might be a good idea to check the room one last time. So we went upstairs and did so. To my surprise we found my jeans (my only pair) hanging on a hook behind the door in the bathroom.

Just before departure we encountered the delightful maid of the Munising Motel in the lobby. Her name is Romaine Perian. We mentioned that a friendly dog had greeted us in our room. She then said, "Oh, there's three of them. They're my buddies." Then she called them. Immediately they appeared from around the corner. Then she fetched a jar of treats, and told her buddies to sit, which they immediately did, and then fed them one at a time. Our two-minute chat with this charming lady was one of the most memorable events of the tour.

On this particular day there were no eating places (that we knew of) on the route. So we decided to carry sustenance with us. We asked Romaine if there was a bakery in town. She directed us to this one, which was only a block away.

Where we stocked up on "lunch food." (The blue banner reads: "Munising, a Great Place to Be." Indeed, it is.)

Much of my lunch came from the "scone case," which contained several delectable varieties.

Day 5 | Munising to Grand Marais

Then we got onto highway H58 and went eastbound out of town. Soon we came to a couple hills. At the top of the second one I said to Bill "That was a pretty long climb." Then out of nowhere came these words: "And there's longer than that coming up." It was from a man standing in his garden, a garden which took up his entire front yard — meaning, the garden *was* his front yard. He was harvesting some of his crops and loading them into a pickup. As for the guy's prediction of the upcoming hills, it turned out that the hill in front of his house was the longest we encountered on the road to Grand Marais.

Not far from the "front-yard gardener's" place we came upon this creatively customized road sign.

We encountered many inspiring sights of wilderness beauty on our tour. This view on H58 is one of them.

Lumbering is a main industry of the U.P. Signs of it appear along H58.

Bill turned down this dirt "truck trail" to heed the call of nature ... and then recognized it was good for a photo.

In this area of the U.P. state campgrounds abound, most of them being located next to a lake.
They've been there for years, as this weathered sign attests.

Day 5 | Munising to Grand Marais

Where H58 intersects road H-52 (also called Cusino Road and also Melstrand Truck Trail) is the town of Melstrand. This is the only town between Munising and Grand Marais. As best we could tell it consists of about two dozen residences and this store.

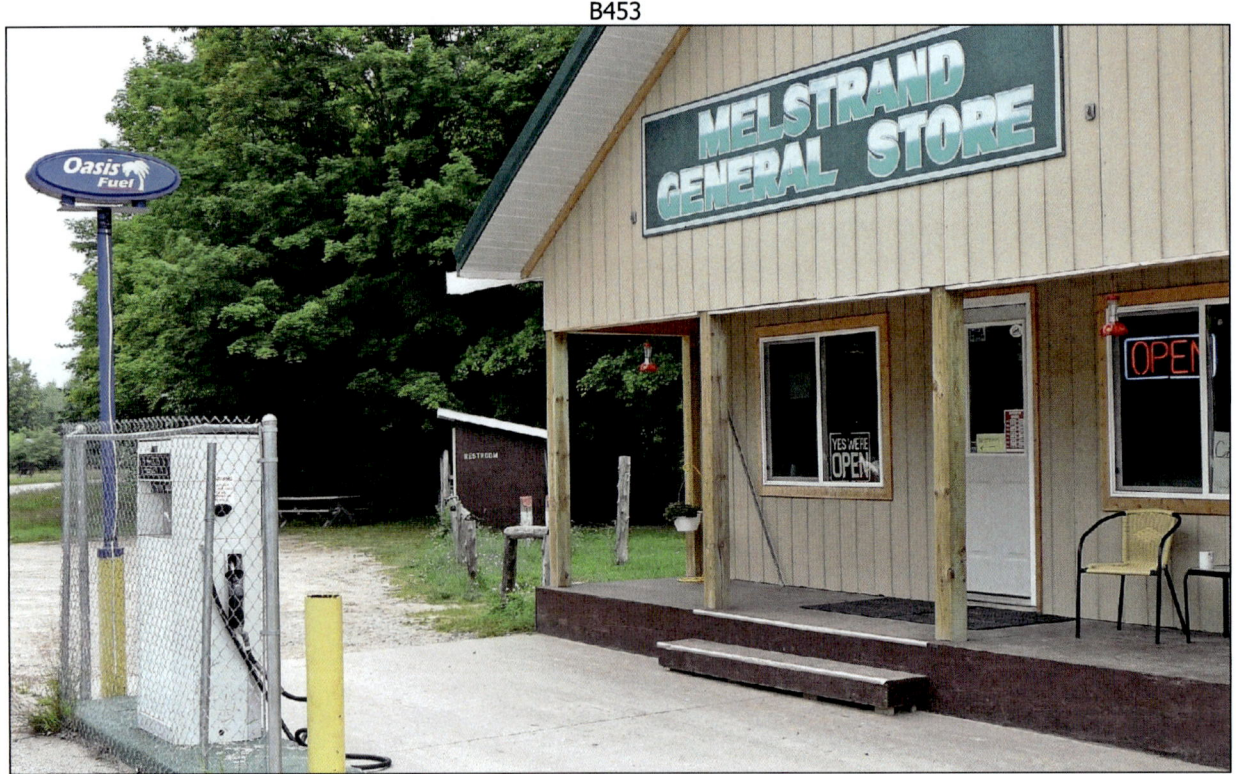

The main commercial enterprise on H58— the Melstrand General Store. We speculated on the purpose of the fence that's on the road side of the gas pump. Was it to block snow plow snow from hitting the pump? Or was it to make cars fill up on the building side? Oh, by the way, the little brown structure in the background is a thoughtful restroom for public use.

Rearward view of highway H58, as depicted in John's bike mirror. This mirror scene — a highway lined by forest, covered by sky, and converging into infinity — I viewed at least a thousand times over seven days.

Day 5 | Munising to Grand Marais

B456

John trying to take a bike mirror photo.
(For this book we used Bill's version of bike mirror photo (B454), as it turned out better than mine.)

B458

Bill's view of the road ahead (photo taken while traveling).

Side-shot of handsome John on the road.

Handsome Bill next to a unique super-tall flowering plant — a Giant Mullein.

B466

Tops of the super-tall flowering plants (of Photo B465).

B467

Giant Mushroom.

Giant Mushroom (of B467) viewed from ground level.

Mailboxes of a small local community (somewhere in the "interior").

Interesting Field filled with St. John's Wort (the yellow flowers).

Close-up of the Interesting Field

Cycling is unique. No other sport lets you go like that — where there's only the bike left to hold you up. If you ran as hard, you'd fall over. Your legs wouldn't support you. — **Steve Johnson**

John's photo of Bill photographing the Interesting Field.

Bill's photo of John waiting for Bill to finish his photographing of the Interesting Field.
(Give us a little extra time and us guys with cameras are "dangerous.")

Wild blueberries abound in the U.P.

Bill in the woods — probably looking for blueberries.

Since our first day of the tour, and especially in the woodsier areas, we kept seeing a certain sight along the shoulder of the road. We speculated on what it was, but couldn't come up with a satisfying explanation. Finally we decided to snap a photograph. Here's what we kept seeing. What do you think it is?

A common sight along the roadside throughout our tour (no, there wasn't two bits beside each one).
It looks like some kind of animal scat loaded with some sort of raspberry-like seed. But what animal? What seed? And why is it repeatedly located along the side of the road?

Bill has a brother Jack who's a professor of entomology at North Carolina State University. Bill sent the photo to Jack. Jack forwarded it to a professor in another branch of the biology department. The fellow identified it as being raccoon scat. Now the only remaining questions are: What plant have the raccoons been eating that resulted in all those seeds? And, why did we see so many of these raccoon stools by the side of the road throughout our tour? (And don't tell me it's because they saw Bill and me coming and we scared the poop out of 'em.)

Along this stretch of road two cyclists — a guy and a gal — zoomed past us from behind. About 20 minutes later they passed us coming back. They were "speed bikers," not tourers — probably staying in a nearby campground and out for some vigorous afternoon exercise.

Day 5 | Munising to Grand Marais

Bill's photo of a guy loading recently-cut logs onto a truck.
These logs were cut somewhere in the "interior" and then hauled to the main road (H58) for trucking out.

John's photo of Bill taking the above photo (B479).
(Hey, I had to do something to amuse myself … can't let Bill have *all* the photographic fun.)

The bicycle, the bicycle surely, should always be the vehicle of novelists and poets.
— **Christopher Morley**   (And, with Chris's permission, we'd include "photographers" too.)

Bill on a Hill. *"It is by riding a bicycle that you learn the contours of a country best."* — Hemingway

At last ... Lake Gitche Gumee! Along one stretch, for a distance of about two miles, road H58 parallels the Lake Superior shoreline. Along this section there's a large, posted scenic overlook. About a quarter mile before we reached it we spotted a break in the trees alongside the road. We decided to take our "Lake Superior photo" there as opposed to the official scenic overlook, which likely has already been photographed about 10,000 times. So we parked the bikes and took the above picture, a view which we now dub for posterity: *Bill & John's Lake Superior Scenic Overlook.*

This time of year in the Upper Peninsula motorcyclists are a common sight. Sometimes you see just one bike with two riders, but most of the time they're traveling in small groups. This was especially the case along highway H58. After taking the Lake Superior photo (B485) we stopped at the scenic overlook to use the facilities. As we were about to depart I noticed a group of four interesting-looking bikers at the far end of the parking lot. I decided, just for the heck of it, to engage them in conversation. So Bill and I peddled over and inquired about where they were from. It turned into an interesting, pleasant chat that lasted about 15 minutes.

We discovered they were from Ontario, specifically the Toronto area. They were on a vacation ride and had been on the road for a number of days. They had been to Wisconsin and Minnesota (or perhaps it was western Ontario and Manitoba) and were now on the return leg of their trip.

Four great Canadian bikers — (left-to-right) Steve Urszenyi, Leroy Thomas, Rick St Jean, Leslie Vine
What's especially cool about these four, at least in my view, is the group's make-up, which includes both racial diversity and gender diversity. Plus, the woman is driving her own "big mean machine." What's more, this diversity extends even to their bikes. Typically in motorcycle groups everyone is riding the same make, like, for example, all Harleys or all BMWs. But with this group, there was one (or maybe two) Harleys and two (or maybe three) non-Harleys. And, the non-Harleys were different makes. These four were truly eclectic — very cool. SIDENOTE: I notice in the photo that each of them has at least one hand resting on their bike — kind of like they and their machine are *one*.

After about 15 minutes we noticed the sky was getting darker and it appeared that rain could be coming. We unanimously concluded that we should be hitting the highway. Leroy summed it up for all of us: "I ain't sugar, but I still don't like riding in the rain."

Bill and I bid them adieu, then mounted our bikes and continued eastward on H58. After about a minute we could hear the sound of motorcycle rumble approaching from behind. Then there was a short horn beep and one bike passed us, the rider waving as he (or she) went by. About 10 seconds later a second flew by, and gave us a wave. Then a third and a fourth, each one giving us a thoughtful parting wave. Bill and I appreciated it. It warmed our heart.

Actually, strange as it might sound, whenever I'm biking I feel a slight kinship to motorcyclists, especially those powered by a V-twin engine. To my mind we share a commonality. We're both riding a two-wheel vehicle. We're both "at-one" with brother wind. And, we're both powered by a V-twin. With them, the V-twin is between their legs; with me, it *is* my legs. I've sometimes wondered whether motorcyclists view me with a similar feeling of kinship. I tend to doubt it. Although I must note that almost every time I've waved to a motorcyclist while on my bike they've nodded or waved back *provided that* there's little or no traffic.

•

Pretty soon we came to a scenic overlook located on Grand Sable Lake. This lake is about two miles from Grand Marais, and rain no longer appeared imminent, so we turned in to admire the view. Shortly, a couple with a dog arrived.

This pooch saw fit to keep Bill under close watch (probably for good reason, although we'll never know for sure).

Soon, they left and then a carload of guys showed up. They piled out to admire the lake. They were from Kalamazoo and were up in the U.P. for a few days, staying at someone's cottage.

When I see an adult on a bicycle, I do not despair for the future of the human race.
   — **H.G. Wells** (Perhaps this is what the doggie was thinking!)

Day 5 | Munising to Grand Marais

Five vacationers from Kalamazoo, Michigan.
In the background is Grand Sable Lake, a beautiful, clear body of water about a mile wide and two miles long.

East end of Grand Sable Lake. This lake is located about two miles west of Grand Marais.

I thought of that while riding my bike. — **Albert Einstein, on the theory of relativity**

B496

One of many impressive Grand Sable Sand Dunes located between Grand Sable Lake and the Lake Superior shoreline.
This dune happens to be across the road from Grand Sable Lake.

B499

Giant Mushrooms by the Roadside.

Day 5 | Munising to Grand Marais

Bill photographing the Giant Mushrooms by the Roadside (B499).

Almost to Grand Marais — just a little farther.

•

Grand Marais is a charming little town with population of about 350. It's located on the southern shore of Lake Superior at the eastern end of Pictured Rocks National Lakeshore. The town bills itself as the "eastern gateway" to the National Lakeshore. The business district is about a block long. This community contains eating places, lodging facilities, and a few stores. At the time we were there a road paving project was underway, which included repaving of the main street through the business district and also paving of a couple gravel side roads.

A main geological feature of the town is a peninsula, called the "north shore," that extends northeastwardly into Lake Superior for about a half mile. This structure results in a bay, called West Bay, that exists between the peninsula and the mainland. At the end of the peninsula is a breakwater and at the end of the breakwater is a light — the Grand Marais Outer Range Light. This bay has been designated as a Harbor of Refuge for Lake Superior sailors. Also at the end of the point is the former Grand Marais Life-saving Station, which is now a Ranger Station. The former keepers quarters for the station is now the Grand Marais Maritime Museum. Bill and I wanted to visit it, but it had closed for the day before we got there. For more on Grand Marais, visit www.grandmaraismichigan.com

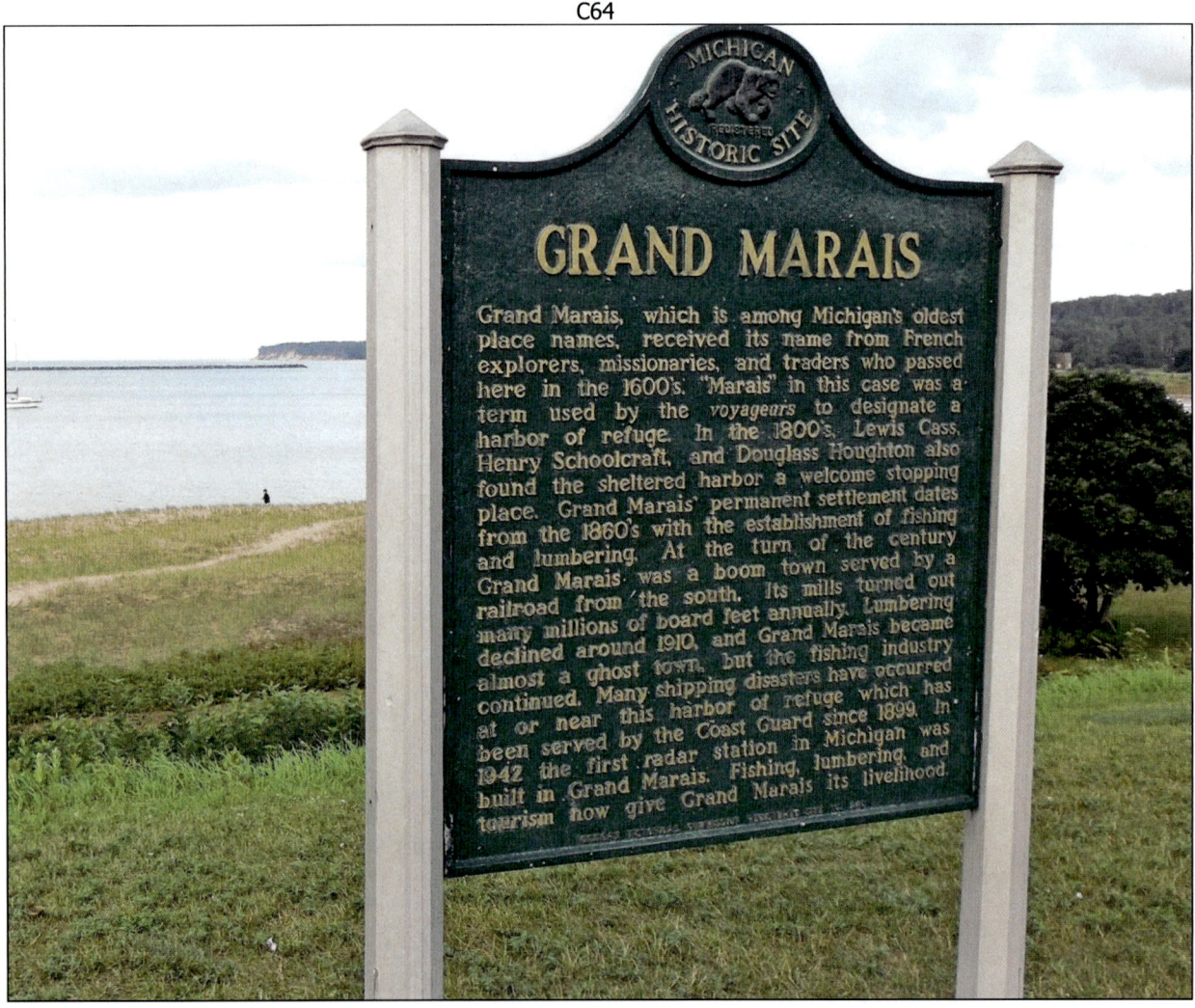

Historical marker located in a waterfront park on the West Bay.

When Bill and I arrived we went directly to our intended lodging. But due to a reservation mix-up the place had no room ready for us. So we left and started biking down the main street. We spotted a road paving crew and asked them for the name of a motel we might stay at. One guy said: "Try the North Shore Lodge. Go to the gravel road that goes out on the north shore point, then go all the way to the end. But you better not wait long because motels are filling up fast." As it turned out, this gravel road is the road that contains the maritime museum and breakwater I previously mentioned. So we peddled to the North Shore Lodge and, fortunately, they had a room available, and a good one at that.

Bicycling is a big part of the future. It has to be. There's something wrong with a society that drives a car to do a workout in a gym. — **Bill Nye, the Science Guy**

Our comfortable lodging for August 6 — on the lakeshore of magnificent Lake Superior.
The sign says the place includes "restaurant and lounge," but, to our disappointment, the front desk clerk informed us that both facilities had been non-operating for the past year-and-a-half.

We went through our usual post-ride ritual of shower, bike uniform washing, donning street clothes, and calling home. Then we biked back into town (about a half mile distance) for sightseeing and dinner. The first thing that caught our eye was the Pickle Barrel House.

How'd you like to live here? Yup, that's right — this is an actual giant barrel that a guy had specially made to live in (see sign on next page).

Day 5 | Munising to Grand Marais

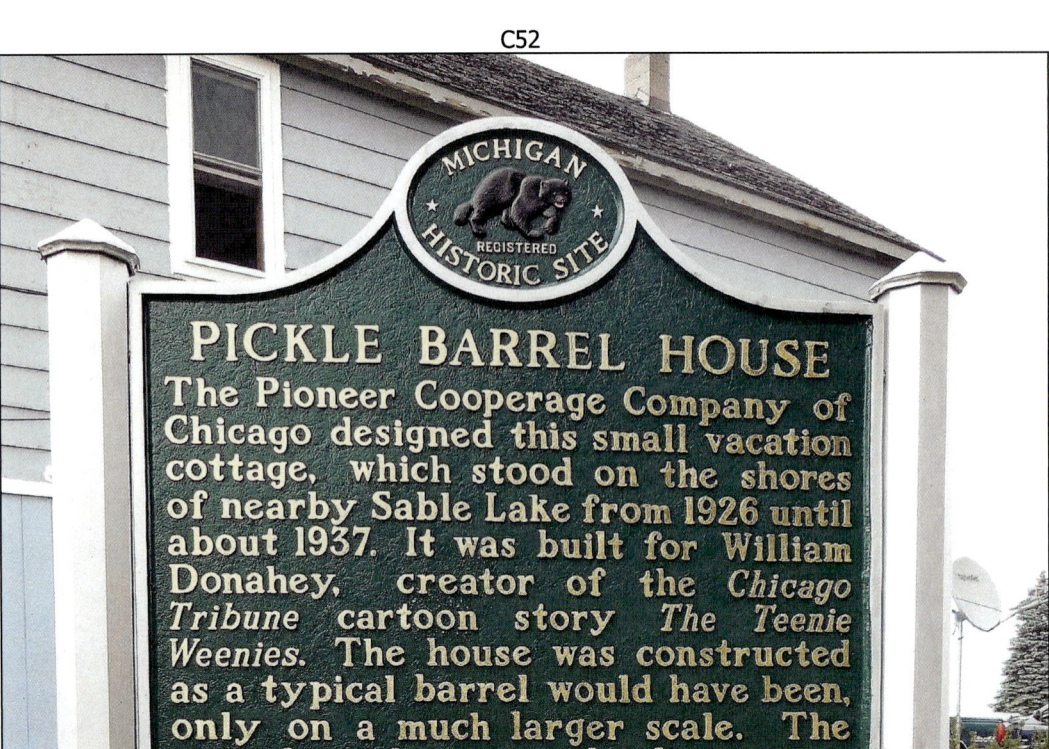

Grand Marais contains several interesting-looking eating places, including one next to the Pickle Barrel House. But for guidance we asked some folks if they could recommend a place. One of them pointed us to the Lake Superior Brewing Company. So we peddled down the block and presented ourselves to the patrons and proprietors of the Brewing Company.

A micro-brewery and restaurant. The parking lot on the side contained a number of motorcycles. The two bikes in front are Bill's and mine.

Inside the Lake Superior Brewing Company.
Bill and I sat at a table along the wall on the left, next to this family of five. By the time we finished dinner the place was filled and people were waiting outside.

Day 5 | Munising to Grand Marais

We shared a pizza for dinner and also had the salad bar. Both were good.

As we were waiting for our food we struck up a conversation with the delightful family sitting next to us. They were from Grand Blanc, Michigan. They were in the U.P. tent camping at one of the campgrounds near Grand Marais. Since the weather forecast called for showers this evening they decided to eat out rather than cook out. One of their family hobbies is birding.

C61

Father Jeff (white shirt), mother Kim (blue shirt), oldest daughter Kaylee (right, in black), middle daughter Ella (middle, in white), baby daughter Clara (left, in pink).
Baby Clara is nine months. She seemed to find me interesting; she's looking at me as Bill is taking the photo. During our meal she would periodically turn around and smile. (In the past couple years, it has seemed like the older I get the more acknowledgement I receive from ladies. I've even now and then had one hold a door for me. Quite baffling, indeed.)

After dinner we walked to the convenience store across the street from the Brewing Company. While we were there a teenage girl walked in, hugging a gallon jar filled with blueberries. Bill asked if he could take a photo of her and her berries. "Oh, no!," she said, "I don't want to be in a photo, but you can take a picture of the berries if you like." So Bill positioned the jar just-so on the store counter and took a photo (C62 next page).

Passing softly through the backcountry [on a bike] creates a fascinating tension. On one hand is the environment, generating powerful swells of energy that course through our psyche. There's something about mountains, deserts, woods that excites us. Yet, on the other hand, the awesomeness of it all diminishes our importance in the earth's affairs. — **Hank Barlow**

Things look different from the seat of a bike carrying a sleeping bag with a cold beer tucked inside. — ***Jim Malusa***

Day 5 | Munising to Grand Marais

"Blue Gold" — a gallon of wild U.P. blueberries, abundant this time of year.
The girl who hand-picked them was proud of her harvest. Undoubtedly she spent more than a few minutes in gathering this treasure. I wonder what her plans were for it. Blueberry pie? Blueberry cobbler? Blueberry muffins? Blueberry pancakes? Blueberry scones? Blueberry yogurt? Blueberry smoothie? Blueberries and cream? Blueberries and ice cream? Cereal topped with blueberries? Blueberries eaten plain from a bowl?

In the convenience store parking lot there was a truck with a unique plate that caught our eye.

"Yes, I'm a Yooper ... and darn proud of it."
And the truck's color? Let's give it a fitting name. How about *Metallic U.P. Blueberry* or *Lake Superior Blue?*

Soon, we started peddling back to the motel. Right where the gravel road turns to go down the North Shore point there's a large boat launch on West Bay. We noticed something unusual. In the parking lot there were no less than a half dozen Michigan State Police vehicles along with a couple Coast Guard vehicles, including at least one with boat trailer attached. A couple hours later that evening we would see State Troopers and Coast Guarders checking into the North Shore Lodge motel.

When we got back to our room we parked our bikes and then walked down to the water for sightseeing. And, of course, we snapped a few photos along the way.

C66

Lovers and Lake Superior at day's end.
Just moments before snapping this photo they were embracing, which likely would have made a more compelling image, but this one will do.

A bicycle ride is a flight from sadness. — **James E. Starrs, The Literary Cyclist**

Long boardwalk to the Big Lake.

John viewing the breakwater and light at the mouth of West Bay.
This bay is a designated Harbor of Refuge for Lake Superior sailors. It has rescued many a mariner from the Lake's fury.

C69

Setting sun with foreboding storm coming in from the northwest.

B503

Same storm as in C69.
The top picture (C69) is mine and this one (B503) is Bill's. Truth is, we didn't set out to photograph the same scene. We were each carrying our camera and using it whenever the whim struck. It just happened that we were both inspired to photograph the same impending storm, but with the inspiration occurring at a slightly different time and place.

Soon after this we went back to our room and called it a day ... and listened to the rain on the roof as we fell asleep.

~ Day 6 ~
Grand Marais to Newberry

DATE: Wednesday, August 7, 2013

LUNCH STOP: Andy's Seney Bar (in Seney)

ROUTE: Hwy 77 south to Hwy 28 — Hwy 28 east to Hwy 123 — Hwy 123 north to Newberry

LODGING: Manor Motel (in Newberry)

TOTAL MILES: 53

When we awoke this morning we found a world enshrouded in grey sky and fog. The rain had gone, but it left us with muddy ground and puddles. Parked in front of the room next to ours was a Michigan State Police pickup truck (below). And, across the parking lot was an Underwater Recovery Unit truck.

C71

Wednesday morning view from our motel room — a foreboding scene.
It seemed like Michigan State Police Troopers and Coast Guarders were everywhere. This Michigan State Police pickup truck was next to our room. The big blue truck in the background is a Michigan State Police Underwater Recovery Unit. A couple minutes after this photo was taken a trooper walked out of his motel room. My curiosity piqued, I stepped out and asked him if there had been a drowning. His reply: "We're looking for someone who came up missing." And that was it, which of course did nothing to satisfy Bill's and my curiosity.

Even though the motel didn't have a restaurant it did provide a free continental breakfast with a decent array of food choices, which Bill and I enjoyed. After breakfast we went back to our room and prepared for departure. We hoped the fog would be lifting soon. But that was not to happen. It just kept getting denser.

We lubricated our bike chains, in preparation for possible rain ahead.

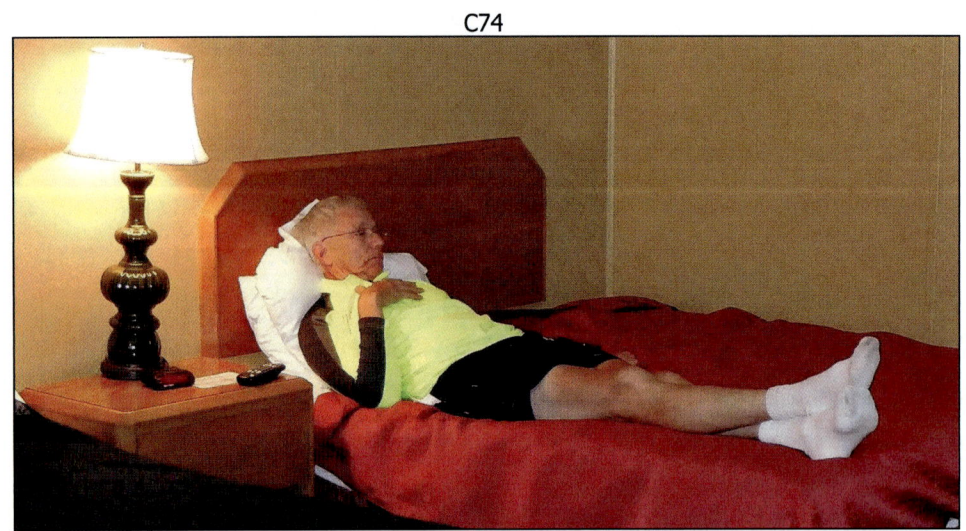

Bill having a catnap before heading out.
For some reason it always took me longer to get ready for travel than it took Bill. So, snoozing is how he often filled his time patiently waiting for me to finish my preparations.

At exactly 8:00 a.m. something surprising happened. An entire road paving crew, with graders, rollers, trucks, asphalt paving equipment, converged on the half-mile long gravel road next to our motel. Surveyors started pounding in stakes and laying out long strings and marking spots on the wet surface with cans of spray paint. And, graders began grading and rollers began rolling, and machines began lining up to lay pavement.

Bill and I pulled out at 10:15. As we peddled down the gravel road past the workers we nodded, and they nodded back. At the end of the road we passed the boat launch. Like the day before, it was filled with State Police and Coast Guard personnel and their vehicles. The fog was still heavy and, so, made us worry a bit about whether cars would be able to easily see us on the highway. But there was an upside to the day's weather. Wind was from the west. Which meant we'd have side wind for the first half of the ride (which was southbound) and backwind for the last (which was eastbound) — or, in short, *no headwind* at any time. After we reached the main street in town we peddled to the end and then onto Hwy 77 south. As it happened, the fog hung with us for the next hour and a half (it lifted about noon), which made for some interesting, or at least different, photo ops — depicted here and on following pages.

B514

It seemed, at the time, that the world consisted only of road, forest, fog … and us.
It was actually *much foggier* than it appears in this and the other photos. In this picture it looks like Bill and I are about a hundred yards down the highway. But, in actuality we're about 50 feet from the camera.

Traffic wasn't heavy, but it wasn't non-existent either. Cars suddenly appeared out of the fog, passed by, and just as swiftly disappeared back into it. At this point I recalled that I had a red light buried in my tool bag. I'd been carrying it for years and never used it. I assumed that probably the battery had expired by now. But we stopped anyhow and I dug it out. To my surprise it worked. So we connected it to the back of Bill's travel bag (my bag had no place for attaching it), set it to flashing, and proceeded on with a slight assurance, or perhaps hope, that it made us more visible to drivers.

It was like biking to Nowhere — we couldn't see far ahead, and neither could the cars that came upon us.
(Looks like this center line has seen rougher days.)

Marsh merged into forest which merged into foggy nothingness — very eerie. It seemed like a headless horseman, or perhaps a headless U.P. Bigfoot, would be charging out at any time.

After being on Hwy 77 for about 20 minutes a Coast Guard vehicle passed us heading northbound. It was a truck towing a boat trailer carrying a big Coast Guard craft. We assumed it was heading to Grand Marais to provide additional "assets" for finding that mysterious "someone who came up missing."

Also, now and then a group of motorcyclists would come upon us. With a couple of these groups the bikers gave us a fist-pump-like wave as they passed. Bill and I wondered why. We hadn't waved at them first. Was it to show a smidgeon of respect, or perhaps a sense of kinship, or maybe to express some "good work, keep it up" encouragement. Whatever the reason, Bill and I enjoyed getting it.

Bill pursuing the Upside to life.

**Along with Bill's many other outdoor pursuits he's also a "birder."
So he stopped to capture this photo of a Gray Jay.**

About 11:30 the fog began to thin out. By noon it would be totally gone and the sun would be shining.

Perhaps it's a reminder, since 1965, that one of the most meaningful parts of life doesn't come from the physical structures we wrap around us but from the camaraderie of family and friends who travel with us.

As you've probably surmised by now, Bill and I, for some reason, find camera photos involving long stretches of highway to be intriguing. Perhaps it's because they seem to capture the essence of what we were doing. We found Hwy 77 to be especially amenable to this type of picture. So here are a couple (more) taken along this road.

Day 6 | Grand Marais to Newberry

Around 1:00 we arrived at Seney, a small town located where Hwy 77 intersects Hwy 28. This also happens to be the northeast corner of the Seney National Wildlife Refuge. On the southeast corner of the intersection is one of the long-time iconic businesses of the area: Andy's Seney Bar. Bill and I enjoyed having lunch there on our 2009 tour and, so, decided to do it again.

The legendary Andy's Seney Bar … it welcomes fisherman, welcomes *everyone!*

This slightly dimly lit establishment looks like it has seen a hundred generations of smoke-filled raucous weekend nights. We perched ourselves at a table and a friendly woman bartender named Shawna came over and handed us some simple menus. Bill and I both ordered the main item on the list — Andy's Half-pound Burger (or maybe it was the "Half-pound Andy Burger"). Anyhow, it was a burger that contained a half-pound of meat. In short time Shawna returned with two plates, each containing a pickle spear, chips, and a monstrous burger.

Bartender Shawna presenting two giant tasty burgers. We chatted with her and discovered she's been working at Andy's for 11 years. Then, Bill and I recalled that she served us our first Andy burgers back in 2009.

Bill and I dug in — yum, yum eat 'em up.

Now let me tell you, there are bar-burgers and then there's this one. If you like bar-burgers you'll think you're in bar-burger heaven at Andy's Seney Bar. This monster was just plain GREAT ... and memorable, too.

Afterward we walked to a bakery café to get a cookie for dessert. It's just across the parking lot from the Seney Bar. We did the same thing in 2009. At that time, while we were standing in the parking lot, who should drive in but Andy himself. Naturally, Bill grabbed his camera and captured a photo. We had a brief conversation with him, at which time he told us he had owned the establishment since 1974.

Andy, proud proprietor of Andy's Seney Bar.

When Bill and I go into a store I often leave my biking helmet on and he often takes his off and hangs it on his bike. On this particular day, he put his helmet on a railing next to his bike before we went into the bakery café. A few minutes later we got back on our bikes and proceeded eastbound on Hwy 28. After we had gone about a half mile Bill says, "Hey, we gotta go back, I forgot my helmet." So we did a one-eighty and started back. After we had gone about 50 yards a car pulls over and stops on the shoulder in front of us. Then a hand, holding Bill's helmet, comes out the window. This nice person had arrived at the bakery the same time we did and, so, when he came out and saw the helmet he knew who the owner was.

The rest of this day's ride, except for the last three miles, was on Hwy 28. It wasn't super busy, but it carried more traffic than we had seen in the prior two days. Depending on where you're at on this stretch of road, the shoulder is either three feet wide or six feet wide. We experienced both. Following are photos we took along this highway.

B541

Hwy 28 in a flatland area, with 3-foot wide shoulder.

B548

Humble abandoned abode of yesteryear.

B551

Snowmobile trail crossing on Hwy 28. The U.P. is a "sno mo haven."

B556

Wheat field in foreground — or is it an oat field? (I'm not a grain expert.)

Side road ... to the U.P. heavens.

Eventually we came to Hwy 123. We turned northbound and peddled three more miles to Newberry and our motel for the night.

The Manor Motel in Newberry — our evening residence on Day 6. It's a well-maintained "traditional-style" motel.

Newberry holds a number of decent lodging establishments, the Manor Motel being one. Another one is Zellar's Village Inn in Newberry and the Comfort Inn on Hwy 28 just three miles south of town. And, there are still more good places, as well. Newberry bills itself as the "Moose Capital of Michigan," although it's not clear how many moose are (still left) in the area. Along with Paradise (Michigan) the town shares the title of "entryway to Tahquamenon Falls."

It also hosts a number of festivals and events during summer and fall. A key feature of Newberry is it's centrally located to many U.P. attractions, some of which are located nearby and others of which you can reach in a 30-minute drive. For more info, visit: www.newberrychamber.net and/or www.newberrytourism.com

Ken Kalin, dedicated owner of the Manor Motel.

•

Bill and I did our post-ride ritual of showering, washing shirt and shorts, donning street clothes, and calling home. Then, for dinner we decided to take a stroll to legendary Timber Charlie's restaurant at the north end of town. On our way we saw two young guys jogging down the side of the street, one of them clutching a case of beer. It looked totally unique. Bill pulled out his camera, but they were intersected by two friends, which caused the four of them to stop and hold a conclave on the spot (in the street), at which point he set down his case of brewski.

How often do you see a spontaneous gathering of friends like this?
(The person on the right is taking the opportunity to re-tie her shoe.)

Day 6 | Grand Marais to Newberry

P135(2009)

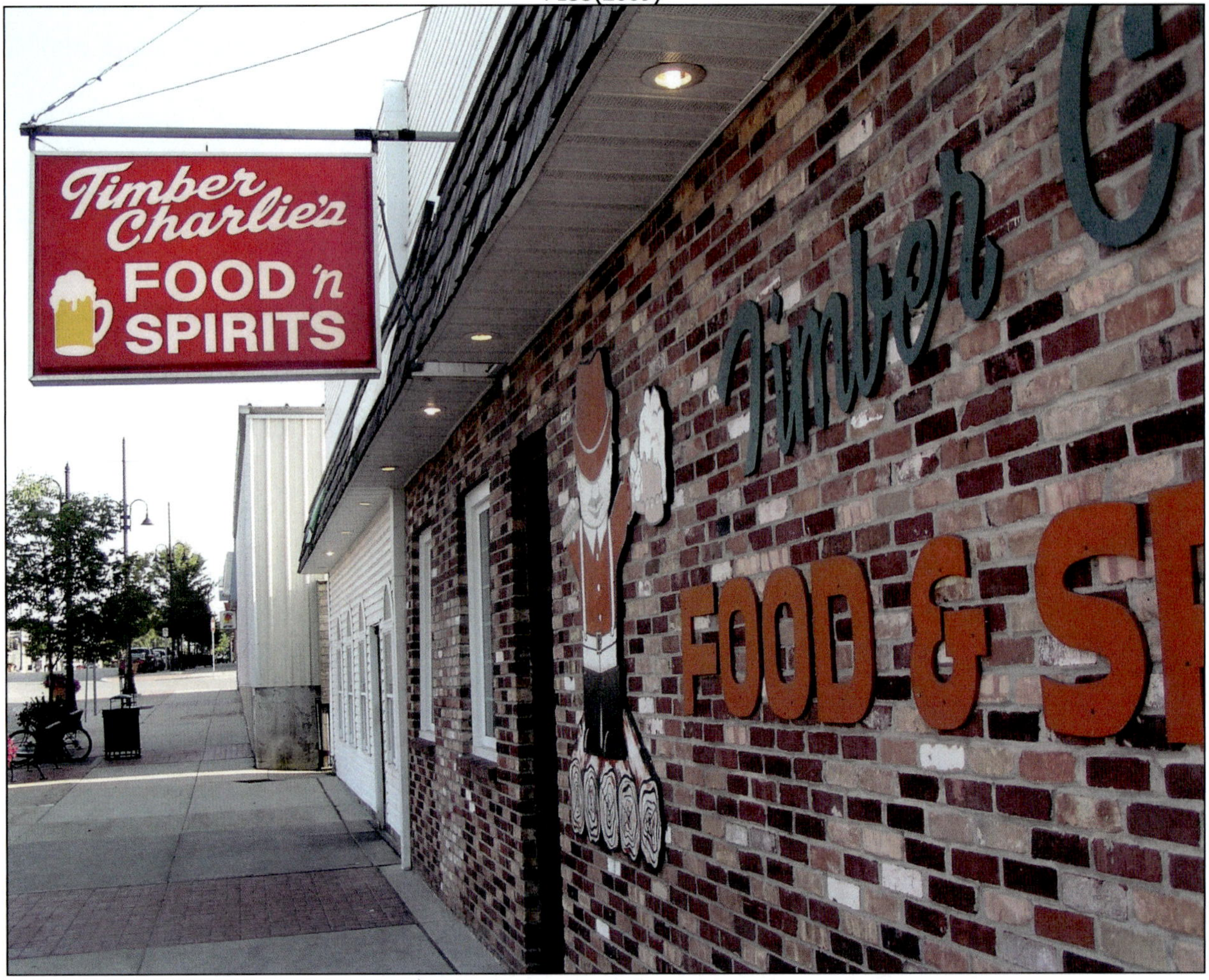

Our Day 6 dining spot — a legendary U.P. restaurant and watering hole.
Bill had a California Reuben. I had macaroni and cheese, which was excellent.

B565

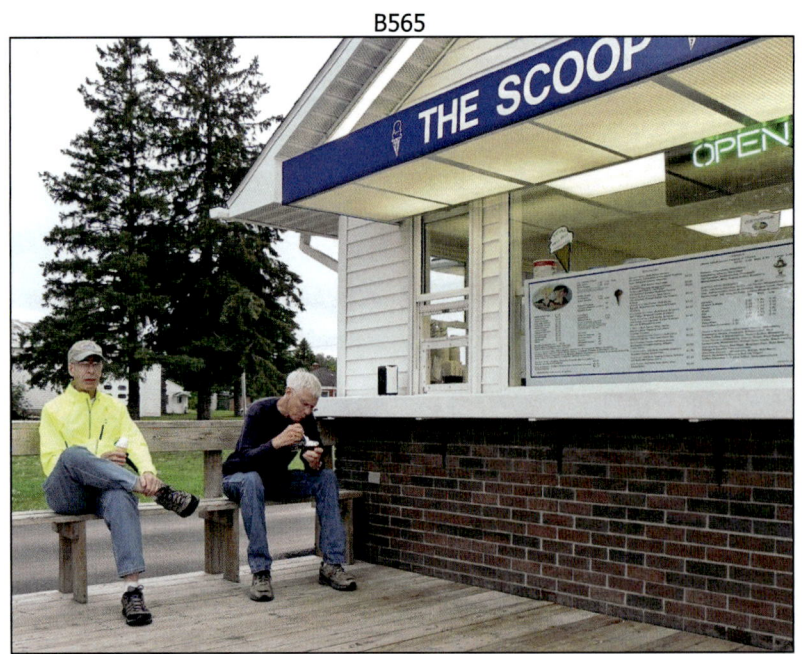

On our walk back to the motel we stopped at The Scoop ice cream stand for dessert.
Then we went back to our room and settled in for a sound night's sleep.

~ Day 7 ~
Newberry to Sault Sainte Marie

DATE: Thursday, August 8, 2013

LUNCH STOP: Roxane's Smokehouse Restaurant (at Strongs Corner on Hwy 28)

ROUTE: Hwy 123 south to Hwy 28 — Hwy 28 east to Hwy 221 — Hwy 221 north to W. 6 Mile Road (in Brimley) — W. 6 Mile Rd east to S. Baker Side Rd — S. Baker Side Rd north to Sault Sainte Marie

LODGING: Bill's Place (in the Soo)

TOTAL MILES: 67

We asked motel owner Ken Kalin what restaurants he might recommend for breakfast. He mentioned several, but noted that Zellar's restaurant is closest. And he added, "They have decent-sized portions, good food, and fair prices." So Bill and I took a quarter-mile stroll to Zellar's.

Motel-owner Ken told us correctly: This place did have goodly-sized portions, tasty food, and reasonable prices.
Zellar's also has a motel facility behind.

I got my usual bowl of oatmeal, which was excellent, and Bill ordered pancakes.

Three giant, tasty pancakes at Zellar's. (If memory serves, it was more than Bill could eat, which is saying something.)

Dean and Jewel Oswald, the husband–wife duo who own the legendary Oswalds Bear Ranch, just a few miles north of Newberry — www.oswaldsbearranch.com

As we were waiting for our food, a husband–wife couple came in and sat down. The man's T-shirt prompted Bill to ask an obvious question: "Are you *the* Oswalds."

"Yes, sir," the man replied. "I'm Dean and this is Jewel." And that began a pleasant five-minute conversation. Bill inquired about how their ongoing legislative effort was progressing.

"Fantastic," Dean said. "The Governor just last week signed the bill making it legal for us to let people touch and hold our bear cubs. We're just thrilled about it." A little later in the conversation I asked if they eat at Zellar's often. "Every morning for breakfast," replied Jewel.

As a side note, Oswalds Bear Ranch isn't a zoo but, rather, is a unique "preserve" for U.P. black bears. They take in orphaned cubs, raise them, and then provide expansive natural-habitat acreage in which to live out their life. If you're one who likes wildlife and finds bears interesting, you'll surely enjoy visiting this place, especially if you're bringing kids along. It's a unique experience.

•

Bill and I were eager to get home to Bill's place before supper. So we departed Newberry at 9:45. The weather this day was sunny, partly cloudy, not too cold, and came with a wonderful five to 10 miles per hour west wind. Which meant we had a backwind for most of the ride home. We enjoyed it, indeed.

Bill noticed that every motel we stayed at for the tour still used the "old-fashioned room key," as opposed to the "new-fangled electronic door card."
We liked using the key; it reminded us of yesteryear.

Three miles south of Newberry, at the northeast corner of the intersection of Highways 123 and 28, is a Comfort Inn. Out front is a moose statue.

Bill and Bullwinkle. Newberry dubs itself "the Moose Capital of Michigan."

At the intersection we turned eastbound onto Hwy 28. After a few miles this caught our eye.

"Think of bicycles as rideable art that can just about save the world." — Grant Peterson

Bill setting up to capture a panoramic photo (this photo by John)

It first happened on our 2009 tour, and it happened again in 2013: On the last day Bill's photographic instincts kicked into high gear. His picture-snapping proclivity and creativity skyrocketed. This began right about now and continued until we got home. So, for the rest of this chapter the storyline (i.e., words) will be minimal and photos will dominate. Also, if it happens that a particular photo "looks different," bear in mind that it's likely not due to photographic sloppiness but, rather, to Bill's picture-taking inventiveness. Now, here we go …

Photo taken on the fly (while Bill was peddling).

B583

Another, taken over Bill's shoulder.
(Speaking of shoulder, along this stretch the shoulder on Hwy 28 was a wonderful six feet wide.)

B589

Doe and Fawn, visiting the "other side of the tracks."
This scene required fast reflexes and zoom — it didn't last long.

I am a cyclist not simply in the sense that I ride a bike, but in the sense that some people are socialists or Christian fundamentalists or ethical realists — that is, cycling is my ideology, a system of thought based on purity and economy of motion, kindness to the environment, and drop handlebars, and a want to convert others. — **Journalist Robert Hanks, The Independent, August 15, 2005**

A group of "fellow two-wheelers" just passed us.

•

At Eckerman Corner, where Hwy 28 intersects Hwy 123 (again), we stopped at an eclectic little roadside store to use the facilities. Bill also snapped a couple photos.

We also met a unique fellow and his dog. As we peddled into the place Bill stopped at the entrance to photograph a rack of furs (B609 next page). I continued up the driveway. In front of the store was parked a small hatchback vehicle. The back hatch was open and standing there was an older man. (You can see him in red shirt in the next photo.) The rear seats in the vehicle had been laid flat and it was stuffed to the top with suitcases, camping gear, and a dog crate containing a small dog. I pulled up and asked where they were going. "Tahquamenon Falls," said the man. Then he said, "Would you know where I could buy a pillow?" I told him the closest place I could think of was Newberry. But he didn't want to go there because it was out of his way.

I asked what he needed the pillow for. He explained that he and his dog "Cooper" were taking a camping trip in the U.P. and that he had forgotten to bring a sleeping pillow and, so, was looking to buy one someplace.

A rack of assorted U.P. fine furs — your choice.

This old man and his dog on a camping trip made me think of John Steinbeck's book *Travels with Charley*. Then Bill peddled up. At this point the man inquired about what we were doing. I told him we were spending a week biking around the eastern U.P. He then asked where we had been camping. I told him we had been staying at motels. His eyes rolled and he sighed and said something about us "not doing it the real way." Bill then responded with unusual candor: "Well, we're peddling 60 to 70 miles a day. When we arrive we're tired, sweaty, dirty ... plus covered with greasy sun block. We don't want to be messing with setting up a tent and cooking food. We just want to shower, get clean, put on dry clothes, and have a relaxing dinner. To our way of thinking, that's 'doing it the real way.'" The man had no reply.

This car, adorned by bear skins for sale, was also in the parking lot. (No, these bears aren't from Oswalds.)

We continued eastward on Hwy 28.

Unique gas station that's getting a fill-up from a gas truck.

The bicycle is the most efficient machine ever created: Converting calories into gas, a bicycle gets the equivalent of three thousand miles per gallon. — **Bill Strickland, The Quotable Cyclist**

Day 7 | Newberry to Sault Sainte Marie

B-11

For this one Bill took two photos (high and low) and "stitched" them together. Bill likes dramatic sky.
(I'm looking in my rearview mirror, probably wondering "what the heck is that Bill up to now?")
You'll note that the shoulder has narrowed to a harrowing 3-feet wide.

B617

As we neared Strongs Corner this sign greeted us. (In Michigan there's no shortage of "capital" cities.)

Day 7 | Newberry to Sault Saint Marie

It was now time for lunch. At Strongs Corner is the venerable Lumberjack Tavern. A hundred yards down the road is a restaurant that had opened in the past year. Bill and I decided to check out the "new guy (or, perhaps more correctly, the new gal) on the block" — Roxane's Smokehouse Restaurant.

B620

The sign's boldness was a big factor in persuading Bill and me to give this place a try.

B622

Majestic sky over Roxane's.
It appears the gods of restaurant success are smiling on this new U.P. culinary venture.

When Bill and I entered the restaurant we were greeted by a cheery, hustling server named Becca. She told us to take any seat we wanted. We did. The dining room radiated a pleasingly bright, colorful, slightly retro ambiance.

Becca promptly gave us menus and brought water (a must for long distance bikers). The menu sported a number of enticing options. We had trouble making up our mind. Then Becca returned and we asked for suggestions. Upon weighing her advice, Bill and I each ordered the pulled pork barbecue sandwich. And, as it turned out, we didn't regret it. If you're ever traveling on Hwy 28 in the vicinity of Strongs Corner, I would suggest you give serious consideration to checking out this place.

B623

Becca delivering Roxane's super-tasty pulled pork BBQ sandwich.
The sandwich was accompanied by French fries and some excellent coleslaw.
It was a lot of food. Bill couldn't even eat all of his.

B629

Roxane's rotisserie barbecue oven —
where select chicken, beef, and pork cuts roast to perfection.

Day 7 | Newberry to Sault Saint Marie

After Roxane's we got back on Hwy 28 heading eastbound. Following are photos we took along the way.

B-10

Snowmobile Trails abound in the U.P. This one parallels Hwy 28.

B638

Lumbering is a major U.P. industry.
One time I saw a sign inconspicuously posted in a U.P. restaurant. I don't remember the exact wording, but it went something like this: *"Are you one of those who doesn't like lumbering? If so, try wiping your butt with a sheet of plastic."*

An engineer designing from scratch could hardly concoct a better device [than a bike] to unclog modern roads — cheap, nonpolluting, small and silent. — **Rick Smith, *International Herald Tribune*, May 2006**

The North Country Trail at a point where it crosses Hwy 28.
The North Country Trail is a meandering hiking trail extending from Lake Sacagawea, North Dakota to Albany, New York. It runs from North Dakota across Minnesota and then Wisconsin, across Michigan's Upper Peninsula to the Straits of Mackinac, down Michigan's Lower Peninsula and into Ohio, then across Pennsylvania and into New York State to Albany. At some points the trail is distinct and easy to recognize. At other points it's nearly invisible.

This particular day was a great "Sky Pic" day.

B645

It was wonderful weather all day long. (Plus we got the 6-foot wide shoulder again.)

B647

A "side shot" taken by Bill, while traveling.

Day 7 | Newberry to Sault Sainte Marie

Eventually we came to a construction zone on Hwy 28. It was about 12 miles long.

Construction worker giving John a wary looking-over.

In some sections we had our own private bike path.

The orange and white cones were our constant companion.

Occasionally John rode behind to capture a photo of Bill.

B660

Eventually the construction zone became a full road again, but without center and shoulder lines.

Soon we came to Hwy 221, at which point we turned northbound. This was the "beginning of the end" — a chain of lesser-traveled roads, which led us into the Soo and to Bill's place. The terrain evolved into more pasture, less woods. Following are photos taken along the way.

B665

Photo taken by Bill as we traveled side by side.

B-12

Probably once a proud farm family's residence, in days of yesteryear.

B677

Junkyards? No thank you. For me it's *Vehicular Field Art* ... of the retro genre.

Mankind has invested more than four million years of evolution in the attempt to avoid physical exertion. Now a group of backward-thinking atavists mounted on foot-powered pairs of Hula-Hoops would have us pumping our legs, gritting our teeth, and searing our lungs as though we were being chased across the Pleistocene savanna by saber-toothed tigers. Think of the hopes, the dreams, the effort, the brilliance, the pure force of will that, over the eons, has gone into the creation of the Cadillac Coupe de Ville. Bicycle riders would have us throw all this on the ash heap of history. — **P. J. O'Rourke**

Bill's a birder. I guess it's "once a birder, always a birder."
(I sometimes wonder what it would be like to be a bird, to be able to spread my arms and glide through the heavens.)

Bill concluding his creative picture-taking at the old Granary building in Brimley, MI.

B685

One of Bill's creative "Granary shots" (of the building in C88 prior page).

B686

Back roads through farmland — we're almost home.

B693

Ah, yes, in the shadow lies the secret.

B695

A touch of "photo-editing zaniness." (Bill's creative instincts eventually had to bloom full-flower at least once.)

Day 7 | Newberry to Sault Saint Marie

Hay barrels in the August sun. The end of summer 2013 in Michigan's U.P. is near.
The chilling winds of autumn are just a few weeks away.

5:10 p.m. August 8, 2013: Home, at last — after seven days, 433 miles.

Nothing compares to the simple pleasure of a bike ride. — **John F. Kennedy**

~ Afterward ~

It seems fitting — after all the planning, training, and actual tour riding — to have a chapter on after-thoughts, a few words about what I gained from it all. Because this second tour derived from the first tour Bill and I took in 2009, that's where I'm going to start.

Discoveries from the 2009 Tour

The seminal tour in 2009 bestowed a number of realizations. First, both Bill and I discovered that we could, in fact, do a bona fide multi-day bicycle tour. Prior to that neither of us were a hundred percent certain we could pull it off. So on the last day of it we were exhilarated. Sure, it wasn't the most grueling bike tour anyone had ever done; we didn't fully "rough it." We stayed in motels, not campgrounds; we ate restaurant food, not campfire meals. And, it wasn't the biggest athletic achievement anyone had ever accomplished; we peddled only 60 to 75 miles per day, not 100 or more. And, we carried only about 30 pounds of gear, instead of the 40 pounds that a typical cross-country biker might carry. Still, in our eyes it was a feat worth being proud of, at least for two casual bikers of ages sixty five and sixty six. So we felt good about it. It lifted our spirits.

Second, to our surprise we discovered that the training was tougher than the doing. Why was that? It's because with the training we would ride, say, a 60-mile distance as one continuous ride, with only three or four short breaks (for peeling a banana, getting out a cookie, taking a pee, etc.). But in the actual tour, covering 60 miles per day didn't occur as one long ride. Instead, it was two 30-mile rides with a 45 to 60 minute lunch break in between: a big difference. Plus, on the tour we were occasionally stopping for five minutes or so to take photographs, something we never did on a training ride. What's more, on training rides there wasn't anyone to talk with, nothing to break the monotony. But on the tour there were frequent conversations. Finally, during training we were riding the same route(s) over and over, thereby viewing the same landscape over and over. But on the tour, every minute of the ride was new scenery. The result: Riding the actual tour involved less physical fatigue and less mental fatigue than doing the training for it. This was a pleasant discovery, indeed.

Third, we discovered that people are intrigued by someone who's doing something different and beyond the norm. I already knew this. And, I had experienced it from time to time. But not in the context of bicycling or an athletic pursuit. I didn't expect that folks would look at Bill and me with admiration, would desire to talk with us, would want to find out about us, and would genuinely wish us well in our endeavor. It was fun and gratifying to experience.

Fourth, I discovered that I enjoy traveling through my home state of Michigan — and, in particular, the northern reaches of it. And, I realized that bike touring is a great way to do it. It enables one to become immersed in it in a way that's not possible when traveling via a self-propelled vehicle.

Fifth, the experience of the 2009 tour reassured and re-convinced me that my "life ain't over yet." Yes, I'm a basically positive guy and I've always (or at least 99 percent of the time) viewed the future in a positive light. But, none of my goals pertained to a physical or athletic achievement until that year. So, planning, training for, and accomplishing the 2009 tour was something that broke new ground for me. It enabled me to accomplish a feat of physical development and expansion. This made it uniquely rewarding and reinforcing. The moment Bill and I wheeled into his driveway on Day 7, I was able to proclaim to myself, to my biking buddy Bill, and to the world — *"WE DID IT!"*

Sixth, I promised myself that if I should ever do another bike tour I would find a way to reduce the constant pressure on the end of my sitz bones (also called sit-bones and butt-bones). This pressure resulted in a pain in my rear for the entire time I was on the bike and also any time I was sitting on a firm surface, such as most restaurant chairs. I resolved to try to find a way to eliminate or greatly reduce this pain. I decided to check out unique bike saddles on the Internet and to investigate recumbent bikes, as well.

Discoveries from the 2013 Tour

Shortly after we had arrived at Bill's place on Day 7 his wife Pam posed a vexing question to me: "Of your two bike tours — 2009 and 2013 — which one was the most memorable and rewarding?" I had no instant answer. Finally I said, "The first of anything is usually hard to beat, because it's an experience you've never had before and, so, it stands alone in its uniqueness. So I guess I'd have to say the 2009 tour was the most memorable and rewarding."

Still, the 2013 Tour was noteworthy and gratifying, as well. In several ways it was a reconfirmation of some of the discoveries of the 2009 tour. Four years had passed since the 2009 tour and, so, neither Bill nor I had the level of stamina we had in 2009. So, completing the 2013 tour was a re-validation that we could "still do it." This, of course, was uplifting.

Also, we learned again that some folks will view with respect and admiration a couple senior guys doing something a little above the ordinary, like a multi-day bike tour. And this was nice to experience again.

And, I rediscovered — or perhaps reconfirmed — that my home state of Michigan is an interesting place to travel and a great state to experience, especially the northern regions of it, where wilderness abounds and traffic is minimal and life seems simpler and values seem purer. I love the Great Lakes waters, and I love the state that borders four of these great waters along 3,000-plus miles of stunning shoreline. The State's motto is: Si Quaeris Peninsulam Amoenam Circumspice, which translated to English says, "If you seek a pleasant peninsula, look about you." I find it to be true advice, so I apply it. In the past 25 years, my wife Janet and I have enjoyed dozens of plays. Of all these plays, my favorite — the one I enjoyed the most and laughed along with the most — was Jeff Daniel's *Escanaba in da Moonlight,* performed in Tawas Michigan by the Tawas Players. I totally enjoyed it. At the end I felt like standing up and shouting, "Yes, THAT'S my Michigan." (Note: this critique pertains to the stage play, not to the movie version of the same title, which I've heard is not nearly as enjoyable as the play.)

But, as a result of the 2013 tour I now have one more play to include in my short list of all-time favorites: *Oklahoma!* by the DeTour Village Players. Indeed, these two plays, both done by "small-town up-north" acting troupes, constitute my two all-time most enjoyable play-attending experiences.

Moving on — another high note of the 2013 tour was that I did the entire 7-day, 433-mile trip with virtually zero butt pain. As explained on the prior page, during the 2009 tour I had a perpetual pain under each of my sitz bones for the entire week. And, so, I had resolved that if I was going to do another tour I would find some way to free myself of this annoying situation. As it turned out, this self-promise caused an interesting discovery in 2013. About six weeks prior to the tour, while nearing the end of a 50-mile training ride and feeling the usual butt pain that had been coming with every such ride, I recalled the 2009 promise I had made to myself. So, when I got home that day I went to the Internet and searched for "the most comfortable bicycle seat for touring." I had done such searching years prior, and had actually purchased, tested, and returned a couple unique (but ineffective) saddles. Still, I decided it wouldn't hurt to go to the Internet again.

The search brought up the usual cadre of "world's most comfortable bike seat" candidates, which I had already seen. But one of the results — www.RideOutTech.com — featured a new saddle, dubbed Green Carbon Comfort seat, which I wasn't previously aware of. So I went to the website and read everything. It included some lab test information that seemed logical to me. So I called the company to order a seat for testing. A woman named Jeri answered the phone. As it turned out she was the inventor of the seat and owner of the business. I placed my order, and she urged me to read all the website info on how to mount and ride on the seat. A few days later the seat arrived. I mounted it on my bike, test rode it, and adjusted it, per instructions. How did it do? It didn't eliminate all the butt pain I was incurring from a 50-mile ride, but it did reduce it significantly. So, the Carbon Comfort seat became my new preferred bike saddle.

The above discovery — a bike seat design that enables doing a 7-day, 433 mile bike tour with reduced butt pain — ranked as one of the highlights of the 2013 tour for me.

But the most rewarding outcome of the 2013 tour came in the form of a new perspective, or new way of viewing and relating to the world. This perspective unknowingly began during the 2009 tour, then went into hiatus for three years, then slowly resurrected during the training months of the 2013 tour, and, finally, came into full flower during the seven days of that tour. I didn't realize what had happened until on my drive home from Bill's place after the tour.

While traveling south on expressway I-75 about 30 miles from the Soo I saw something far down the highway. At first it looked like debris. Then I noticed movement. As I got closer it looked like an animal wrestling with a carcass in the middle of the highway. Finally, when I got so close the creature couldn't stay any longer a giant bald eagle leaped skyward and took to flight on powerful huge wings. It was a stunning sight. Then, at that very moment something surprising happened. A certain reflexive thought-sequence shot through my head: "This is *special* ... quick grab the camera ... get a photo ... how am I gonna take this photo...." My foot moved automatically from accelerator to brake. I looked to the right to see how I could pull off onto the shoulder. Then I realized that this unique "bald eagle on I-75" event couldn't be captured in a photo because the eagle would be gone by the time I could stop and get outside the car with the camera. So I steered back onto the highway.

It was then that an epiphany struck: I realized that I was relating to the world the way I had been relating to it for the prior seven days. I was viewing it as a collection of special events, things, and beings waiting to be discovered, experienced, recorded, and remembered.

This realization gave me pause. After reflecting on it for a few moments I realized that the enjoyment and memories that I had captured from my prior weeklong biking experience had resulted, in large measure, from my holding this perspective during that time. Because of this perspective the entire seven days had been infused with deeper joy and expanded meaning.

Then the final part of this epiphany happened. I realized that this viewing of the world as a collection of special things waiting to be discovered, experienced, recorded, and remembered was a perspective that could be extended beyond that of a bike ride. Perhaps I could use it to enhance any particular day of my life ... perhaps I could us it to enhance my *entire* life. And, so, this realization was the biggest reward I took away from the 7-day bike tour of Michigan's Eastern Upper Peninsula in August 2013 with my friend, and avid amateur photographer, Dr. Bill Bacheler.

When the spirits are low, when the day appears dark, when work becomes monotonous, when hope hardly seems worth having, just mount a bicycle and go out for a spin down the road, without thought on anything but the ride you are taking. — **Sir Arthur Conan Doyle, January 18, 1896, Scientific American Magazine**

She who succeeds in gaining the mastery of the bicycle will gain the mastery of life.
— **Frances E. Willard**

It would not be at all strange if history came to the conclusion that the perfection of the bicycle was the greatest incident of the nineteenth century. — **Anonymous**

I started biking to condition my body. Then I discovered, my spirit was being conditioned, as well. — **John Correll**

# # #

Mackinac Bridge — a.k.a. Mighty Mac — gateway to Michigan's magnificent Upper Peninsula

Mighty Mac in the Mist

Made in the USA
Monee, IL
22 October 2021

3a42554a-92f8-4624-a63c-51040111b40aR01